PELICAN LAGOON
RESEARCH CENTRE

KANGAROO ISLAND

POCKET NEXT PAGE

THE ECHIDNA
AUSTRALIA'S ENIGMA

MELVILLE ISLAND

Darwin •
ARNHEM
LAND

KIMBERLEY
PLATEAU

NORTHERN
TERRITORY

QUEENSLAND

BURNETT

Brisbane •

ULURU

WESTERN
AUSTRALIA

SOUTH
AUSTRALIA

NEW SOUTH
WALES

MURRUMBIDGEE

Sydney •

• Perth

ACT

CAMBERRA

Adelaide •

VICTORIA

Melbourne •

TASMANIA

PELICAN LAGOON
RESEARCH CENTRE

Hobart •

KANGAROO ISLAND

THE ECHIDNA
AUSTRALIA'S ENIGMA

Dr. Peggy Rismiller

HUGH LAUTER LEVIN ASSOCIATES, INC.

CONTENTS

ACKNOWLEDGEMENTS

First and foremost I would like to thank Lucas, Sonic and Knuckles. This book happened because computer game characters sparked the fantasy of a young mind to learn about the real beasts. Thanks to Hugh Levin, the publisher, for taking a personal interest in the subject and to Jeanne-Marie P. Hudson, the editor, for her untiring assistance. I appreciate the time and effort contributed by science editor Dr. Joe Merritt, critical review of the manuscript by monotreme colleague Dr. Peter Temple-Smith and comments on presentation from Jim Roberts.

Many people contributed to the realities contained in this book. I am especially indebted to Echidna Earthwatch team members, the Australian Trust for Conservation Volunteers, Echidna Care, many students, friends, and the greater community who have contributed moral support and tens of thousands of hours to this study. Without the assistance of this extended Team, results presented here would not have been possible. The "We" mentioned throughout this book refers to that Team. The Center for Field Research, private corporations, conservation agencies, numerous small businesses, and individuals have provided the technical and financial support for the volunteers and my ongoing echidna research at the Pelican Lagoon Research Centre on Kangaroo Island. Thanks to all of you! A special thanks to the Department of Anatomical Sciences for supporting me as a visiting research fellow and to all of my colleagues at the University of Adelaide for their encouragement.

I would like to thank the curators and collection managers in the anthropology and mammal departments of the South Australian Museum for access to off-exhibit materials. A special thanks to Neville Pledge for guidance and assistance about fossils and Gondwana history.

Finally, a very special thanks to the dedicated perseverance of my partner, wildlife photographer and biologist Mike McKelvey. Over the past ten years, we have experienced together many magical monotreme moments and Mike has captured some of these to share with you. All images were taken working with animals in the wild and represent years of preparation, waiting and learning.

PREFACE

For over a decade I've been peering under bushes, hiding behind trees and roaming the woodlands, shrublands, swamps and coast of Kangaroo Island, Australia. I have also had the opportunity to work in different parts of mainland Australia from the cooler highlands of Tasmania, the arid zone of western central Victoria and the Dividing Range of Queensland. My subjects are active at all times of the day and in all types of weather, so where they lead I have attempted to follow. This is a book about the short-beaked echidna*. It is not a definitive biology book, but an echidna biography including cultural and biological facts, plus a little bit about me as a field biologist and other people who help with our research. It is annotated with true tales from the field, supplied by volunteers and researchers. Throughout the book are findings of other dedicated echidna researchers from the past 200 years. Readers can find additional information, both general and specific, from books and publications listed in the bibliography.

Watching an echidna in the wild is an experience that one never forgets! The purpose of this book is to introduce people to the world of the echidna, their incredible history, remarkable life and fascinating environment. Primitive mammals? Echidnas live solitary lives, are slow moving, insect eating and egg-laying. They have acute hearing, sensitive smell, are masters of camouflage, accomplished escape artists and decidedly inquisitive. They maintain low population numbers, are broad-spectrum foragers, physiologically adaptable and not aggressive toward other wildlife. As a member of the oldest surviving group of mammals, the echidna is a living model for sustainability. For me, this weird, whimsical and timeless creature is a constant reminder of nature's wonders and living proof that facts can be more fascinating than fiction.

Dr. Peggy Rismiller
Pelican Lagoon
Kangaroo Island
Australia

*The short-beaked echidna is a protected species throughout Australia. All research undertaken by the author and volunteers was conducted in accordance with permits issued by the Department of Environment and Natural Resources, South Australia. Animal ethics approval was granted by the University of Adelaide, Adelaide, South Australia.

(Above) Kangaroo Island tiger snakes, Notechis ater niger, *are not always black, as their Latin name implies. They can range in colour from pure black to chocolate and bronze-brown. The belly scales may be black, grey, white, red or yellow.*

(Opposite) Kangaroo Island is a biological window. With habitats ranging from semi-arid to temperate rainforest, it is the continent's third largest island. Influenced by both the Indian and Pacific Oceans, the island still treasures its mysteries both beneath and above the sea.

SETTING THE SCENE

THE LONG ROAD TO AUSTRALIA

I have always been curious. My mother says I entered the world not with a demonstrative wail, but with an assertive "Why?" From earliest memory, nature, especially animals and more specifically reptiles, fascinated me. The second of four siblings, I was the one who brought home bugs, tadpoles and snakes from the time I could walk. Fortunately few of the snakes in rural Ohio, where I grew up, are venomous and I survived to discover the other wonders of nature.

At sixteen, restless and stifled by high school, I applied to become an exchange student and escape my final year. My first country of choice was Australia, home of big reptiles, pouched mammals and the elusive egg-laying echidna. I was sent to the country of my second choice, Germany, and remained there a number of years. After a few twists and turns I studied biology at the Goethe University in Frankfurt. Under the guidance of Professor Gerhard Heldmaier I discovered the significance of sound biological methodology, the broad horizons of basic biological research and the complexities of dynamic biological interactions. His holistic approach of combining physiology, ecology and environmental cues continues to influence my research perspectives today; in order to understand how an organism functions, you cannot separate it from its surroundings. After 12

(Above) Working in a natural environment is a privilege, a pleasure and a challenge. After a decade of continuous field research with the solitary-living echidna, I have gained new perspectives reinforcing the dual role of researcher and pupil.

(Below) Each day of field-work generates immense amounts of data. To keep up with the paper work, field assistants take their office into the field. Solar energy powers portable computers, data loggers, flatbed scanners and office equipment for innovative solutions to new jobs.

years at university, I had more than a doctorate degree. I had learned that inconsistencies may be part of an organism's make-up. I had also learned to trust my observations, to question theory and to meticulously document unexpected happenings. I was restless to move on. Australia, land of the giant reptiles, was still looming. Meeting Dr. Roger Seymour, lecturer at Adelaide University on sabbatical in Germany, gave me the opportunity. On 2 January, 1988, I arrived in Australia with two partial grants. I was to work with tiger snakes and echidnas, a live-bearing reptile and an egg-laying mammal!

Reading the available literature on echidnas did not begin to answer all my questions. Basic biological questions asked over 150 years ago had not been conclusively answered. One of my first jobs was going into the field and finding echidnas with an egg in the pouch. A biologists heaven or hell? What began as assisting with a field project examining energetics of echidna eggs became a vocation. Some actually say it is my obsession. The intricacies of echidna life style and biology had me hooked. Here was a challenge, an environment and a purpose that captivated my imagination and energy.

NATURE'S LABORATORY

Kangaroo Island, Australia's third largest island, is situated off the coast of South Australia in the Southern Ocean. It lies within temperate waters and has a Mediterranean climate. Biologically it provides a series of ecosystems between the continental extremes of alpine and desert. Being in close proximity to Adelaide, a university town, Kangaroo Island offers exceptional opportunities for field research, such as mine. I anxiously anticipated my first visit.

Most species of wildlife on Kangaroo Island also occur on the mainland. However, wildlife on Kangaroo Island behaves differently than on the mainland because of a significant factor: habitat. After official settlement in 1836, colonists recognised the need for shelter belts, retaining corridors and islands of native vegetation. Today about 27% of the entire island is conservation land and more is protected in

Mathew Flinders named Pelican Lagoon after colonies of nesting birds when he discovered Kangaroo Island in 1802. Today the estuary is an aquatic reserve providing fish nurseries and key habitats for rapidly disappearing species of marine plants and animals.

private holdings. A major factor influencing Kangaroo Island's intact habitats is the absence of introduced rabbits and foxes.

Kangaroo Island has a rich biodiversity, which we call "A Biological Window Into the Past." Travellers, nature enthusiasts and scientists visit the island to experience unique ecosystems. It is an environment where native plants and animals occur and interact much as they did 200 years ago. Many of the island's 1,800 species of plants, the backbone of habitat, have disappeared or are greatly restricted on the mainland. Working in the low impact habitats on Kangaroo

11

(Above, left) Kangaroo Island geology includes evidence of the ancient super continent Gondwana as well as ice ages, plate tectonics and recent fault activity. The land is a link to understanding habitats. Coastal areas are often considered in terms of economic or aesthetic value. In reality these are critical systems forming the natural lifebridge between land and sea.

At the time Europeans discovered this large island it was uninhabited by native people. Explorers learned that the wildlife was not afraid of humans and was easily hunted. Thankful for the food, they named this place Kangaroo Island in honor of the largest land mammal they found. Today, two species of macropods are native to the island, the Western Grey Kangaroo (right) and the smaller Tammar Wallaby.

Island can be at once daunting and mind-boggling. People who have experienced impacted habitats are often unprepared for the richness of the island ecosystems. Here are habitats in which the chemical and physical relationships between plants, animals and the micro climates are so interwoven that they cannot be separated.

From early times, Kangaroo Island has played an important role in echidna research. It began in 1884[1] when the pair of echidnas caught "in copulation" and taken to the South Australian Museum in Adelaide produced an egg. In 1978 the Kangaroo Island echidna, *Tachyglossus aculeatus multiaculeatus*, was recognised as a subspecies of its own. Mervyn Griffiths wrote "Kangaroo Island echidnas [are] the most distinctive of all echidnas with their very long fine pelage obscured by a plethora (overabundance) of characteristic extremely long thin spines.[2]" From the 1950s through the 1980s numerous echidna researchers have come here to work.

In 1988 both the echidna and Kangaroo Island found me. I moved to Pelican Lagoon on the east side of the island where biologist and photographer Mike McKelvey had established a research centre. Our shared love of nature formed a lasting bond. Living and working in the field, we initiated the first life study of short-beaked echidnas from egg to adult.

Island habitats provide unique lifestyles for many native species. Within woodlands, dense vegetation provides abundant shelter and food for brush tail possums (above). Echidnas (opposite, right) can be found in all types of native habitat around Australia. Present numbers are unknown but they inhabit areas from the coast to alpine regions and from desert to rain forest.

(Right) Kangaroo Island temperate waters are high in biodiversity. This is home for many unique species and the last habitats where some marine organisms still coexist. The Australian spectacled pelican, common on the continent, is the largest of the world's pelicans.

IN THE FIELD

Since 1990 the base for my echidna ecology research has been the Pelican Lagoon Research and Wildlife Centre. Here, sustainable research and living go hand in hand. The privately owned centre is operated as a Land Trust established upon environmentally sound principles and is self-sufficient in energy and water. It utilises solar power for all electrical needs of researchers and volunteers. It is a place of ideas and doing, not of manmade things. Due to the fragility of the land and our conservation ethics for sustainable practices, only small numbers of people work at the research centre at any one time.

Volunteers are the mainstay in the long term echidna research[3] and maintenance of the centre. Who are these volunteers? They are local and international people of all ages and from all walks of life. Very few are scientists. All are concerned, enthusiastic people who want to invest their energies in the future of the environment. Volunteers contribute more than 14,000 hours annually to echidna field research[4]. They are trained to assist with tasks as diverse as radiotracking, biological surveys, data input, information dissemination and the management of feral species.

Coastal areas around Pelican Lagoon are spectacular, but present special challenges for echidna researchers. Animals shelter in the natural caves and beneath salt depressions or subterranean lenses of fresh water, all of which distort or block radio signals from tracking transmitters.

One of the first challenges of an echidna field biologist is to find an echidna. Depending on the time of year and where you are in Australia, echidnas are active both day and night. In the 1800s scientists employed Aboriginal people who found echidnas with dogs at night[5]. We have worked with Aboriginals to learn their ways. For long-term studies we have developed different methods of finding echidnas. Although our methods may take longer, they are productive. We not only find animals, but we have also gained additional insights into their behaviour and ecosystems. We have also learned different approaches to sustainable research.

Echidnas roam over great distances through all types of habitats, follow no set movement patterns and cannot be lured into traps. On top of that they are masters of camouflage. Not only in colour and shape, but also in disposition, the echidna is in tune with its surroundings. At the Kangaroo Island study site our highly motivated volunteers search an average of 300 hours on foot before making their first initial contact with an echidna. Most searching is done during daylight and even with all senses alert, you have to be in the right place at the right time to find an animal. Tired feet, numb fingers and sun-burned noses acquired during this long and tedious task are quickly forgotten when one of the elusive creatures is found and brought in.

We weigh, sex and code all new animals. A radiotransmitter is attached to all females and selected males and subadults. In most species, transmitters are attached to a collar fastened around the neck. Echidnas have virtually no neck, and with their spiny coat, fitting a collar is out of the question. Instead, a case containing the transmitter is attached to the spines on the back with fast-setting epoxy glue. A few spines are cut for the procedure, but this does not hurt the animal as spines are modified hairs. When the battery needs to be changed after nine months, we simply unscrew the canister and exchange the transmitter.

Transmitters are used for relocating animals in the field. That is not always as easy as it sounds, especially with echidnas. The closer a transmitter is located to the ground the more restricted its transmis-

Mallees are a special type of eucalyptus tree. They do not lose all their leaves at once but shed constantly through-out the year. The litter protects the tree roots from drying out and provides habitat for many animals.

Between 1950–1973 vast areas of Kangaroo Island were cleared for agricultural and economic development. Today, 25% of the island is a resource bank for natural assets and future growth. Local and international communities are investing time, money and land to secure resources. Eucalyptus (top) and Donkey orchids (bottom) are a part of the island's natural resources being conserved as our environmental capital.

sion. As natural diggers and underground dwellers, echidnas go into caves, under tree roots, deep into soil litter, sand dunes and below salty surfaces or snow fields. All of these conditions can distort, reduce and sometimes even eliminate a radio signal. Echidnas have taught us tracking tricks that manufacturers of transmitters never dreamed of. I tell all volunteers that when you learn to track an echidna successfully, you can radio track anything that lives above the ground.

ECHIDNA NUMBERS AND DISTRIBUTION

From a geographical point of view echidnas are Australia's most widely distributed native mammal[6]. They are found from coastal areas to inland deserts and from rain forests to above the snow line. Due to their wide distribution, echidnas are perceived as "common," yet no one knows how many there were at the time of European settlement or how many there are today.

Several historic records give us insight into what is happening with echidna populations in specific areas of Australia. In 1884 William Caldwell[7] went to the Burnett River region of Queensland and removed 1300 to 1400 echidnas in a two-month period. Seven years later, Richard Semon returned to the same area because of their apparent abundance. In five months during 1891 and 1892, Aboriginals collected 464 echidnas for Semon. This is only one third the number that Caldwell found[8]. Recent community monitoring through Echidna Watch recorded fewer than 50 sightings in this area in a two-year period.

In the late 1960s, Mervyn Griffiths reported from the Australian Capitol Territory (ACT), "During October and November echidnas in the ACT cease to be cryptic and invade the suburbs of the city of Canberra. The reason for this is quite unknown but it is of considerable help to us in planning our work to know that a good supply of echidnas will be available at that time. In one memorable week in October 1967 we took 19 echidnas from Canberra gardens and streets

(Above) As a monotreme, the short-beaked echidna belongs to the oldest surviving group of mammals but we still do not know its lifespan, when it becomes sexually mature or how often it breeds in the wild. Volunteers from around the world invest energy and time to answer basic biological questions.

(Right) Field research in natural habitats, such as this island wetland, provides a sound base for endangered species programs.

in response to telephone calls from householders. The animals were of various sizes and were nearly all males.[9]" This "invasion" of echidnas did not continue and has not been observed since 1968.

Griffiths also worked with echidnas on Kangaroo Island. He did not use radiotelemetry, but relied on finding known echidnas in the same area each year. He wrote, "Recently in one week, Oct 26–Nov 3, 1973, 35 echidnas were taken on Kangaroo Island. Twenty of these were female." During the 1990s we returned to the same area three different years. We searched for the same amount of time and on the same dates as Griffiths. Our maximum number found was eight animals, compared to Griffiths 35. We have documented similar declines throughout Kangaroo Island.

People often ask me if the echidna is endangered. In reality a lot of facts are needed before this can be determined. For many, "endangered" implies that there is only a very small number left in the wild. Criteria used to assess the status or vulnerability of a species include age of sexual maturity, frequency of breeding, litter size, juvenile mortality, number and distribution of animals in the wild.

Echidna numbers and density cannot be assessed using traditional mammal survey techniques. They are not attracted to baits or record-

17

Documenting the life history of an animal means following its natural cycles and being prepared to work at any time of the day or night. Echidnas change their activity patterns to avoid heat and to take advantage of the life cycles of their food sources.

ings, they do not have home dens or follow regular paths and they cannot be trapped. Our studies show that number of digs cannot be equated to echidna numbers. Presence or absence of scats cannot be used reliably as a monitoring technique to determine if echidnas are even in the area, as they simply disintegrate during the rainy season.

A community-driven continent-wide survey, Echidna Watch, is contributing information on echidna sightings from around Australia. This survey records a lot of data including where, at what time of day and in what type of habitat people are currently seeing echidnas. Life studies in the wild are providing factual material to begin assessing many biological questions. Together, community and science are providing essential background for assessing the vulnerability of this species. Is the echidna endangered? Further studies in different parts of the continent will be needed before we have a realistic answer.

In the 1990s echidnas are still officially considered 'abundant' on Kangaroo Island, even though data show there have been distinct impacts on population numbers. Nonetheless, Kangaroo Island is geographically distinct and has suffered fewer impacts than many parts of the mainland. It remains one of the best places in Australia to work in naturally evolving ecosystems and learn about echidna population dynamics today.

BIG MAMA, VOLUNTEERS AND SERIOUS SCIENCE

Can serious science be conducted with the aid of volunteers? Yes, of course! More than 20 years of working with people has taught me that every volunteer has something to contribute. My task is to recognise each individual's skills and talents and introduce them to new tools and resources relevant to the work that we are undertaking together. This investment of my time is proportional to what I get back. Shared perspectives result in volunteers working until the job is done, carrying on through all types of field conditions when others

would have quit and making discoveries that others would never have seen.

Some researchers find it difficult to take animals named Big Mama, Curry, and Spike seriously. Why? As much as with apes[9] and elephants[10], echidna names are important to the people who work with them. Volunteers play a vital role in searching for echidnas and they name any new animal they find. Sometimes an echidna's character prompts the name. Spike was extremely prickly. Food and field work go hand in hand, as is reflected in echidnas named Curry, Pasta and Muffin. Each animal has a distinct personality. Digger did just that when he was discovered. For me, each name carries a lasting impression of the significance of a volunteer's contributions to science.

Newly found echidnas are also marked with colour codes, inconspicuous colour tubes placed on the spines of designated body parts. YTL for example is Yellow Tail Left and RSR is Red Shoulder Right. This gives us a visual code to identify the animal in the field and in records. A tiny electronic tag or transponder with a ten-digit number/letter code is inserted under the skin as a life long positive identification. They are read using a hand held scanner.

Since our humble beginning with two animals and two transmitters, over 90 individuals have been found and coded at the Pelican Lagoon study site. Not all of these have transmitters. Even with volunteer assistance it is not practical to keep track of that many echidnas. We do believe that the entire adult population in the primary study area has been found. This is based on the fact that all new or unmarked animals found in recent years are subadults, newcomers to the area. Interestingly, there is a sexual bias of two males for every female in our adult population.

Without volunteer assistance we would not be able to keep track of key individuals such as Big Mama, relocate her when she sheds her transmitter, document her mating, gestation, and growth of her puggle, secure milk samples, find her nursery burrow, monitor feeding intervals, plot foraging patterns, determine lactation duration, follow the young's establishment of a home range or ascertain its fate. Following known individuals, our global team of volunteers is leading the way in verifying, clarifying and substantiating facts and fiction about the elusive echidna, one of the planet's longest surviving mammals.

During the past decade, Earthwatch members and other volunteers have provided thousands of hours of observation and dedication to aid our research. Their contributions have bridged gaps between our knowledge and the world of the echidna. Insights from their perseverance have given us new perspectives on survival.

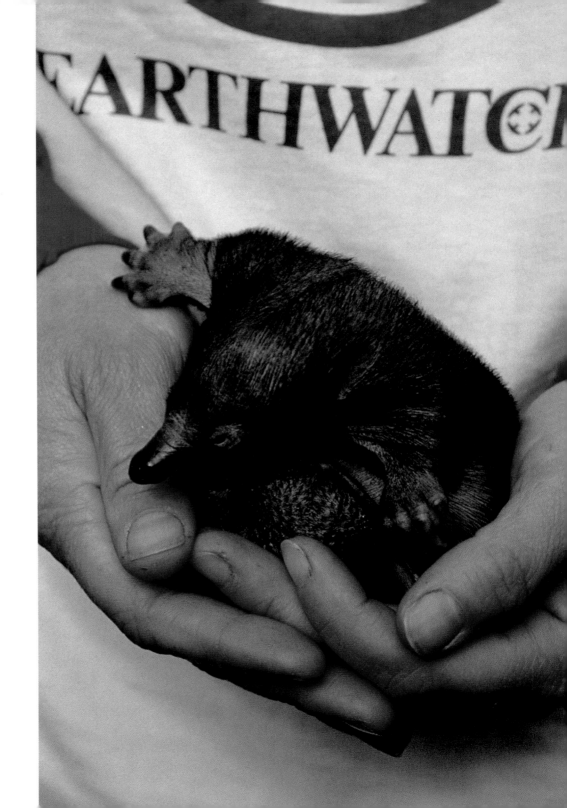

THE ECHIDNA CHRONICLES

GONDWANA—LAND OF THE GONDS

About 570 million years ago, long before the dawn of mammals and at the time when invertebrates, animals without backbones, were first appearing, there was one very large continent straddling the equator. It is now known as Gondwana—land of the Gonds[1]. This supercontinent included what is now Africa, South America, Australia and Antarctica. Pieces of Europe and Asia surrounded Gondwana as small islands. Movement of landmasses related to convection of the earth's semi-liquid mantle caused earthquakes, floods and reshuffling of boundaries. Readjustment of the earth's crust caused a drifting away from the equator. When winged insects began appearing about 300 million years ago, continents were uniting. Direct connections were established between the landmasses of Gondwana and northern continental fragments including North America, Siberia, Europe and parts of Asia. Australia shifted southward in close proximity to the south pole.

Land movements during the Triassic, 245 million years ago, heralded the appearance of the dinosaurs and the beginning of a great separation. Gondwana itself began breaking up in the early Cretaceous, about 140 million years ago. Now began the era of the monotremes—the egg-laying mammals. As India broke from Africa, Australia and Antarctica began drifting north. During the late Cretaceous, placen-

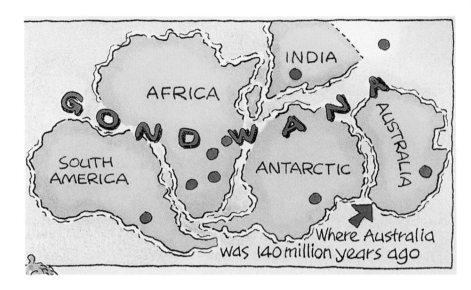

Australia, New Zealand, Africa and Antarctica were all once part of the super-continent we call Gondwana. As the land-masses separated, about 140 million years ago, the monotremes, or egg-laying mammals, appeared. Few monotreme fossils have been found to date. There are fossils of other mammals from this time period but none are living today.

tals, live-bearing mammals whose foetus is nourished through the placenta, and marsupials, the pouched mammals, began to appear. At this same time, New Zealand broke from Antarctica and later Australia followed. Continental separation lasted nearly 100 million years. During this time unique groups of mammals were evolving, each occupying their own niche.

MONOTREME LEGACY

Taxonomists use fossils to identify ancient plants and animals and determine how they fit within groups living on our planet today. The broadest biological classification is the Kingdom. Each of these groups is further broken down into Phylum, Class, Order, Family, Genus and Species. A Class indicates groups of animals or plants with generalised similarities. Mammals are one Class of animals; they all have hair and suckle their young. The first mammals emerged about the same time as the first dinosaurs, nearly 245 million years ago. None of these are alive today.

We currently recognise 26 living Orders of mammals. Echidnas belong to the oldest Order, Monotremata. This name was coined in

24

1803 by the French evolutionist Etienne Geoffroy Saint-Hilaire. He
tried, unsuccessfully, to establish the echidna and platypus as a new
Class of mammals. He did not believe they were primitive or inferior
to other mammals, but that their differences from both mammals
and reptiles were significant. The word Monotreme comes from two
Greek words, *mono* meaning "one" and *tremata* meaning "hole."
This refers to the single opening, the cloaca, through which urinary,
faecal and reproductive products all pass outside of the body.

Until the 1970s, the history of monotremes was virtually unknown.
Significant fossil discoveries then shed light on this ancient surviving
group of mammals[2]. First, scientists found three teeth of a 25-million-
year-old platypus called *Obdurodon insignis* (*obduros*, Greek, meaning
"enduring", in reference to the teeth being permanent and *insignis*,
Latin, meaning "distinguishing mark," this being a significant discovery). Soon after this discovery, a complete skull of a younger species,
Obdurodon dicksoni, was uncovered. Next, scientists found an opalised
jaw fragment with teeth at Lightning Ridge, NSW. The fossil was
identified as belonging to a monotreme which was given the name
Steropodon galmani (*sterope* and *odous* from Greek meaning "flash of
lightning" and "tooth"). Some years later, the jaw of a second distinctly different monotreme was identified and christened *Kollikodon
ritchiei*. The name refers to the bun shape of the molars and to Alex
Ritchie of the Australian Museum who persuaded the Lightening

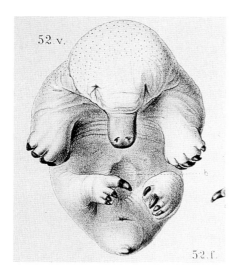

52. v.

52. t.

(Above) The cloaca, the "one hole" for which the Monotremata were named, is clearly evident in Richard Semon's 1892 illustration. Urinary, faecal and reproductive tracts all join internally in the urogenital sinus and are excreted from the body through the cloaca.

(Right) The protruding eye of an echidna is large and well-protected by long eyelashes. The flat cornea and position of the eye probably give echidnas a panoramic view of the world. Moving through the dense understorey and across difficult terrain, they exhibit excellent depth perception and peripheral vision.

Ridge opal miners to share the fossils they unearthed. Both fossils date back 120 million years! Monotreme lineage continued when the age of the dinosaurs ended 65 million years ago. Echidnas and platypuses inhabiting Australia and New Guinea today represent the oldest surviving mammals on our planet.

ABORIGINAL PEOPLES AND THEIR LEGENDS

Hominids, precursors of modern-day humans, first appeared in Africa about 4.4 million years ago. The oldest human remains, found in a cave at Gran Dolina, Spain, date back 800,000 years[3]. There is still a lot of conjecture about when humans first set foot on Australian soil. Some anthropologists, scientists who study ancient people, believe that certain groups of Aboriginals, indigenous Australian peoples, arrived as long as 120,000 years ago. Aboriginal people lived in small groups, moving between regions as the seasons and food sources changed. Echidnas lived throughout Australia and were used as a food source. Whereas some Aboriginal people praise the delicate flavour of echidnas, others say they are eaten only in time of need as the "steaks" are little and the animal is very fat.[4]

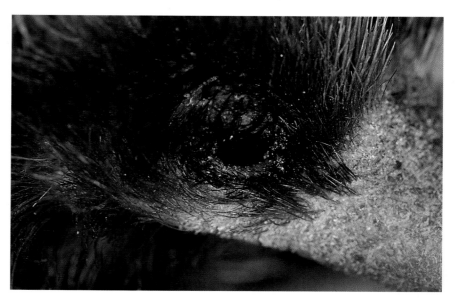

(Above) The prominent grooming claw on the hind foot is one characteristic used to distinguish sub-species. In this Tasmanian echidna, both the second and third claws are elongated. Grooming claws are effectively used for scratching or removing annoying ectoparasites like ticks.

(Right) One secret behind the echidna's great strength lies in its skeletal structure and muscle attachments. The leg bones are short compared to other mammals and the large shoulder girdle is more like that of a crocodile than a mammal. This arrangement gives the echidna a huge mechanical advantage for digging and lifting.

There are very few rock drawings of echidnas. Two better known ones are in the Quinken Galleries at Lakefield National Park in Queensland and at King Edward River Crossing in the Kimberley Ranges of Western Australia. These rock paintings may be more than 9,000 years old. Echidnas play a small but notable role in Aboriginal stories. Some of these traditionally oral histories have been documented in books. Traditional Aboriginal stories tell about creation, life and how one should live. There are many accounts relating how the echidna got its spines. Stories from different peoples are not exactly the same, but all include aspects of water, swallowing (ie. the eating of flesh), spearing and personal relationships.

This is a traditional story from the Dalabon people, Arnhem Land: "Echidna had a child that was too young to be left alone. It was placed in care of Tortoise, who was the mother's mother. When Echidna returned it discovered that Tortoise had swallowed the child. A fierce fight broke out. Echidna struck Tortoise with a stone–which stuck to the back and became the shell. Tortoise threw spears that stuck in Echidna's back. Tortoise then took to the water and now lives in the shell that remained upon her back. Echidna

The unorthodox design of the echidna pelvis allows the hind leg and foot to reach practically any part of the body. The hind feet are rotated outward giving the appearance of "being backwards." Many museums in the world have skeletons with the echidna feet directed the wrong way!

stayed on land and recovered from her wounds. The spears remained as spines on her back."

This story was recorded from a member of the Arunta people in Arnhem Land:
"Echidna became very jealous and mistrusting when his wife left him. He tracked her and sat outside her camp with his back against a porcupine bush (spinifex). Evil thoughts consumed him so that he did not notice the sharp points of the grass sticking in his flesh. After a month he left his hiding place and the points remained.[5]"

WHAT'S IN A NAME?

The Echidna, oft called *Tachyglossus*
Short and dumpy and not a colossus.
He wanders around with his beak to the ground
After insects beneath rocks and mosses.
—*Earthwatch volunteer, Robert Bender, 1991*

In 1791 the H. M. S. Gorgon left Port Jackson, New South Wales to sail back to England. On board were undescribed specimens of animals from the recently colonised land of Australia, then called New Holland. Among these unusual creatures was a spiny, stout, beaked mammal with the accompanying note "captured on an anthill in New Holland." And so the first echidna was transported to Europe to be described in scientific literature.

Naturalist George Shaw of the Royal Zoological Society in London was presented this mammal with a bird-like beak and long pointy spines. Since it had no teeth, a long tongue, and was found on an anthill, he thought it might be related to the South American ant-bear or perhaps was a new genus of porcupine. With some reservations, Shaw likened this Australian creature to the anteaters, and consequently named it *Myrmecophaga aculeata* (*Myrmecophaga* = ant-eating, *aculeata* = spiny) and published his findings in 1792.

28

Ten years later, in 1802, anatomist Everard Home discovered similarities (the urogenital sinus was a major common feature) between the echidna and the platypus, *Ornithorhynchus paradoxus* (*Ornithorhynchus* = birdlike snout, *paradoxus* = a paradox, something that seems contradictory). Because of the close relationship, Home suggested that these animals be placed in the same Order. He further recommended that the scientific name of the spiny Australian creature be changed to *Ornithorhynchus hystrix* (*hystrix* referring to the uterus and to similarities in the reproductive organs of the echidna and platypus).

Aboriginal artist Bluey Roberts is known for the details included on his exquisite hand-carved emu eggs. This design shows a serpent surrounding an echidna, a goanna, a fish and a long-neck turtle (opposite side). Ants embellish one of the many distinct layers of colour in the shell.

Soon after, the genus name was changed to *Echidna*. A fitting name derived either from Ekhidna, a Greek goddess who was half reptile and half mammal or *Echidnos* which means "spiny," and is Greek for hedgehog. Alas, the genus name *Echidna* had already been assigned to a group of spiny fish in 1788. Finally in 1811, after several more changes, the spiny, beaked creature was given the genus name *Tachyglossus*, which means "swift or rapid tongue" and the species name *aculeatus*, which means "with points." Although sometimes referred to as "spiny-anteater," Echidna has remained the common English name for this incredible mammal.

MONOTREMES AND OTHER MAMMALS

There are three subclasses of mammals: Monotremes, Marsupials and Placentals. Monotremes are different from other mammals, as they lay and incubate eggs to give birth to their young! Domestic mammals and most native mammals in the northern hemisphere are placental, having an embryo attached to the maternal tissue or placenta. The marsupial or "pouched mammals" give birth to lesser developed young which continue their development in the pouch or marsupium. Marsupials are most common in Australia, but some are found in South America and one species in North America.

There are only three living Monotremes, the short-beaked echidna, called simply echidna, the long-beaked echidna, which today lives only in Papua New Guinea and the platypus. Platypuses live in the eastern states of Australia including Tasmania. The short-beaked echidna can be found in areas throughout Australia with one subspecies represented in Papua New Guinea.

The echidna is playing a significant role in the renaissance of contemporary Aboriginal art. Artists are now incorporating the echidna into designs on pottery, jewellry and textiles. Echidna objects made of glass, brass, silver, wood, stone, wool, pewter, clay, cloth and even opal are part of my collection. (Painting © WIGGII 92)

MONOTREME TAXONOMY

Class	Mammalia	Mammalia	Mammalia
Subclass	Prototheria	Prototheria	Prototheria
Order	Monotremata	Monotremata	Monotremata
Family	Tachyglossidae	Tachyglossidae	Ornithorhynchidae
Genus	*Zaglossus*	*Tachyglossus*	*Ornithorhynchus*
Species	brujnii	aculeatus	anatinus
Common name	long-beaked echidna	Short-beaked echidna	platypus

A subspecies is a division within a species. Unlike true species, these animals can interbreed, but have distinguishable appearances or reside in different geographical locations. Until more DNA work is done, we currently recognise five subspecies of echidnas[6], *Tachyglossus aculeatus.*

Subspecies	Geographic location
T. aculeatus multiaculeatus	Kangaroo Island
T. aculeatus setosus	Tasmania
T. aculeatus acanthion	Northern Territory and Western Australia
T. aculeatus aculeatus	Queensland, New South Wales, South Australia, Victoria
T. aculeatus lawesii	Papua New Guinea

Seldom seen in captivity or outside of local village markets in the highlands of New Guinea, the long-beaked echidna is a species which may disappear before we learn about its basic life history.

Distinguishing characteristics are the degree of hairiness, length and diameter of the spines and the grooming claws on the hind feet. Tasmanian echidnas, which may live year-round in a cool climate, have short spines and long soft pelage. Those living in consistently warmer parts of Western Australia have long spines and very little hair on the back. Most echidnas in Victoria and New South Wales have very stout spines and dense dark hair.

I'M NOT A HEDGEHOG AND MY SPINES AREN'T BARBED

Early European settlers arrived in a far away land filled with a strange flora and fauna. When a plant or animal had even a vague resemblance to something "back home," it was given a familiar name. This is why echidnas are still referred to as hedgehogs, porcupines or even porkys in some parts of Australia today.

One of the most commonly asked questions is: "Are echidnas related in anyway to the porcupine or hedgehog?" The answer is simple:

33

Platypuses and echidnas are the only egg-laying mammals. Echidnas live on land. Platypuses live and feed primarily in fresh water. They naturally inhabit rivers and streams of eastern Australia and Tasmania.(Animals/ Animals, Photo © Hans and Judy Beste)

No!! Porcupines belong to the Order Rodentia or rodents. Their relatives are guinea pigs, chinchillas and rats. Porcupines are wide-spread and inhabit North and South America, Europe, Africa and Asia. They have teeth and love to chew. Their diet includes bark, roots, tubers, bulbs, seeds, leaves and sometimes insects. Quills of New World porcupines are hollow and barbed. These sit loosely on the surface of the skin with the small barbs acting as effective grippers. If a predator gets too close the quills stick in their skin and detach from the porcupine. The barbed quills work into the skin at a rate of 1 mm/hour, causing death if vital organs are punctured.

Hedgehogs are related to moles, shrews and tenrecs in the Order Insectivora meaning insect eaters. Hedgehogs are well known in Europe, but different genera, genetically related groups, can be found in Africa, the Philippines, Sumatra, Egypt and the Gobi desert to northern China. The European hedgehog was introduced to New Zealand and is now endangering some native birds and insects! Hedgehogs have tiny sharp teeth and voracious appetites. Their diet sometimes includes frogs, snakes, lizards, young birds and mice, as well as insects. Short spines covering their backs are not barbed and cannot be released as a defense mechanism. Hedgehogs can roll up, protecting their face and presenting predators with a pin cushion-like ball. Echidnas can also roll up, but prefer to dig straight down into the ground, presenting only a spiny back.

An echidna, porcupine and hedgehog placed side by side look nothing alike. The spines of an echidna are distinctive from those of the hedgehog or porcupine. They are not barbed, have different lengths and thicknesses on different parts of the body and are firmly anchored in the skin. Individual spines can be moved independently of each other using a special layer of muscle in which the spines are rooted. Both porcupines and hedgehogs have small, button-like noses. The echidna's birdlike beak is part of its skeletal structure. It is covered with tough, hairless skin, where the true beak of a bird is covered with a horny cuticle. All three mammals walk on four feet. But, the hind feet of two (like most other mammals) point forward—

(Above) Hedgehogs occur in many parts of the world, but not in Australia. These insectivores or, "insect eaters," are related to moles and shrews. They are not related to the echidna (Animals/Animals, Photo © Robert Maier).

(Right) Porcupines are rodents related to guinea pigs and rats. They have teeth for chewing bark, roots, seeds, leaves and sometimes insects. Their barbed quills sit loosely in the skin and can painfully stick into flesh or anything that bumps into them (Animals/Animals, Photo © Gerard Lacz).

not the echidna! Its hind feet are turned outward and rotated backwards.

Many authors use the term 'spiny anteater' and echidna synonymously. Are echidnas truly anteaters? Pangolins and aardvarks are anteaters. Probably the best known is the giant anteater which ranges between southern Belize and northern Argentina. All these mammals eat ants and termites, some rather exclusively, but the most distinguishing characteristic of this group is the drastic reduction, or total lack of teeth. Spiny anteater or not, the major difference between the anteater, the porcupine, the hedgehog and the echidna is that the former are placental mammals and the echidna is a monotreme, one of only three egg-laying mammals in the world!

ENIGMATIC ICON

From cave walls in the outback to billboards in the cities, from quiet, ignored bush gnome to Olympic 2000 mascot, the echidna, its status and recognition, plods onward. Australian flora and fauna represent

a major socio-economic resource that is used to attract people from around the world. Traditionally, marsupials and some birds have been used to represent Australian products and companies. Kangaroos and koalas abound on items from aeroplanes to tea bags. The marketability of the echidna is just making a debut.

In 1966, when Australia changed its currency system from pounds to dollars, the echidna was immortalised on the five cent coin. Despite being carried in the pocket of nearly every Australian, it was 20 years before the echidna began to show up on the logos of grass roots organisations and friends clubs. Slowly but surely Australian companies, artists and crafts people are recognising the captivating aura of the echidna.

Echidnas have wangled their way into the competitive world of advertising. From underwear (called Antz Pantz) to mining (echidnas are the original 'diggers') and wine (we do recognise echidnas as cultivators of the soil), the echidna can be found representing

Australian products. Even prestigious car companies are using the image of the echidna to reinforce their message, "If you don't adapt, you won't survive!" Not big, bold and beautiful, but tenacious, versatile and full of intrigue, the short-beaked echidna, a plodder and ancient survivor, represents the spirit of Australia. Not many icons can boast a 120 million year ancestry.

(Above) By studying the internal organs of echidnas and platypuses, Everard Home discovered that these two mammals are related. He published his findings and this illustration of one of his specimens in 1803.

(Opposite) Echidnas can be found from coastal habitats to alpine snowfields, in deserts and rainforests. They are highly mobile and inquisitive. Subadults may travel over 40 kilometres from their nursery area to establish home ranges they may use for more than 40 years.

VIVE LA DIFFERENCE

That youngish echidna called Timmy
Had lips most remarkably skinny.
No pucker, no pout and nary a shout
To attract the female echidninny.
—*Earthwatch volunteer Hester Bell, 1993*

MONOTREME EXTREMES

Echidnas epitomise mammalian anomalies. They have many features common to mammals: mammary glands, hair, four appendages and a lower jaw consisting of a single pair of bones. However, assemblage and modification of these traits make echidnas significantly different. They do not have a nipple or a teat, but still suckle their young. They have no teeth and the mouth opens no wider than the width of the tongue. Some body hairs have been transformed to a shield of spines. Their hind feet are rotated backward, and to top it off, echidnas produce young by laying an egg! A weird mixture of mammal, reptile and 100% monotreme, the echidna is a mammal with a difference.

Since its discovery, the echidna has intrigued all those who have seen it. In February 1792, while moored in Adventure Bay, Van Dieman's Land, now known as Tasmania, a ship's officer, George Tobin, wrote

"The only animals seen were the kangaroo and a kind of sloth about the size of a roasting pig with a proboscis two or three inches in length...On the back were short quills like those of the Porcupine... This animal was roasted and found of a delicate flavour[1]."

SIZE OF A DINNER PLATE

How big is an echidna? Many people have described them to me as, "small, medium, large or average." Others compare the echidna to a well-known and loved object, the Australian football, or the size of a dinner plate. Two of the more unusual descriptions have been "size of a potato" and "big as a wombat!" It is difficult to assess the size of echidnas because they can roll into a perfectly round and spiky ball or flatten out long and narrow to bask in the sun. On top of this, adult echidnas are somewhat like adult humans; there are big ones and small ones.

Throughout Australia, adult echidnas weigh 2.5 to 7 kg (5.5 to 15.5 lbs) and measure between 30 and 45 cm (12 and 18 in) from tip of snout to tip of tail. On Kangaroo Island the largest echidna we've ever found was a female weighing 5.5 kg (12 lb). The smallest sexually mature female in our study population weighs only 2.5 kg. There may well be geographical differences in echidna sizes that are not yet documented. Individuals in the wild show seasonal fluctuations in body weight.

ANATOMICALLY CORRECT

QUILL OR SPINE?
Some of the echidnas finest points are noticeable at first glance, namely its spines. Spine and quill are sometimes used synonymously in echidna literature, as well as in dictionary definitions. This has raised the question: Do echidnas have spines or quills? Going to the root of the question, I discovered that confusion runs deep. According to Australian morphologists Baldwin Spencer and Georgina

Using beak and claws to expose galleries of ant eggs, an echidna will rapidly draw food into its mouth with the spiny tongue. The beak is used to rupture insects and larvae that are too large to ingest whole.

(Above) Echidnas use their spines as extra "fingers." The spines, individually controlled by special muscles, help an animal to right itself, to climb up the fork of a tree or scale slippery rocks out of a water hole or cave.

(Right) Spines occur in distinct rosettes on the head, sides and tail. When disturbed or agitated an echidna will erect all the spines, pull its head under the protective covering and present a defensive appearance.

Sweet, researcher Mervyn Griffiths[2], and others[3,4,5], echidna spines are modified hairs. "Each hair or spine in cross-section, at the appropriate level, consists of external and internal root sheaths, a keratinized cuticle, a cortex and a central medulla...[6]"

In Australia's Macquarie Dictionary the 4th definition of quill is "one of the hollow spines on an echidna." Biologically, a quill is defined as: 1) a hollow shaft, 2) the hollow, horny barrel of a feather and 3) one of the hollow sharp spines of a porcupine[7]. Macquarie defines spine as: "a pointed process (natural outgrowth) or projection, usually of a bone" and "a stiff, pointed process or part on an animal, such as a quill on a porcupine, or a sharp, body ray in a fish's fin."

Confusing, yes. However, the hair-splitting conclusion of biologists working with echidnas is that the stiff, pointy outgrowths or rods on an echidnas back are spines.

Because spines are modified hairs, they are occasionally shed. Echidnas in the wild do not go through a complete moult each year but a certain number of spines are replaced, mainly in spring and summer. By placing colour codes on different parts of the body, we have learned that the smaller spines on the head are shed most often.

Some colour codes put on the larger flank or back spines are still there after ten years. Some captive echidnas shed large numbers of spines. This could be due to many factors including diet, exercise or stress.

Another interesting point about echidna spines is their long (1.5 cm or 5/8 in) root that goes through the skin into a special muscle layer. This muscle layer allows the echidna to individually control movement of the spines. It is not yet conclusively resolved if this muscle is plain or striated[8]. When threatened, an echidna may only erect the spines on the head, while others on the body are still lying down. When the echidna is in grave danger or annoyance, all spines stand erect.

Spines also act as "extra fingers." In our limestone country there are many natural solution tubes. These pipe-like channels connect the ground surface with subterranean passage ways and caverns which echidnas frequent. We regularly observe troglodyte echidnas using their spines to help grasp and push their bodies upward much like a rock climber in a chimney climb. We have also seen echidnas climbing out of the water between rocks, or going up between the forked branches of a tree. Sometimes they fall over backwards putting themselves in a vulnerable position. With 'spine power,' flexing the spines

on the flanks and back and pushing against the ground, the echidna rolls itself over on all four feet again.

We do not understand the protective role of spines during bushfires, but echidnas are often seen with melted spine tips. After a fire passes we move into the field to learn what is happening. When we locate a transmitter signal buried in a fire area there is always the question: Is the animal alive? As much as twenty-four hours after the main fire has passed we have watched echidnas dig their way out of the dirt and ashes, then proceed to forage amongst charred stumps and smouldering debris. This kind of observation has led us to work with physicists, chemists and medical researchers.

INTELLIGENCE

Examining the skull, people are amazed to find echidnas have a very large brain cavity. How brainy are echidnas? Because "primitive" has also been perceived as "not bright," this issue has challenged scientists over the decades. Harvard anthropologist Stephen Jay Gould expounds on the myth of echidna primitivity and scientific prejudice in his essay "Bligh's Bounty[9]." Learning abilities and intelligence of echidnas have been tested using maze running as well as positional, visual and tactile experiments. According to Othmar Buchmann and Julie Rhodes, zoologists from the University of Tasmania, echidnas learn quickly and improve performance with practice. There is evidence that they store, classify and integrate information they receive. "The results obtained (in instrumental learning of echidnas) compare favourably with such mammalian species as cats and rats[10]" write Buchmann and Rhodes.

More than size, the structure of the echidna brain is remarkable. The neocortex, the site of "higher mental functions" equals 43% of total echidna brain weight[11]. Supposedly, the greater the neocortex volume, the "more advanced" the animal. The nearly spherical, richly convoluted surface of the neocortex is also significant. Traditionally this complexity, round with folds, has been used as a gauge for mental advancement or intelligence in mammals[12].

44

The echidna uses its keen senses for finding food and avoiding unwanted encounters. The beak may be lifted to sniff the air or lightly tapped on the ground to feel vibrations. Spines around the sensitive ears adjust to focus on surrounding sounds.

From field work, we have assessed how well echidnas learn and remember. When a road-injured echidna was brought to the research centre, it was lethargic and nonresponsive. We held it in a container for monitoring, and each time food was offered, a cue was given by tapping two rocks together. After a few days the echidna was transferred to a large outside holding facility. When the rocks were tapped, the echidna appeared and was given food. After three weeks it was fully recovered and released. Even five years later, this echidna continues to appear out of the bush when it hears "the cue." This experiment has been repeated with other individuals using cues over varying lengths of time. All echidnas quickly learned to respond to a cue and retained the response for many years.

Ears

Most echidnas lack an outer ear or pinna. I have seen only a few mainland echidnas with a flap of skin around the ear and it looks strange indeed. An outer ear could be disadvantageous when pulling the head back under a spiny shield for protection. Despite absence of a pinna, the echidna has excellent hearing. The large ear slit is surrounded by finer spines than on other parts of the body. These can be moved to protect the opening or help direct sound. According to researchers Michael Augee and Brett Gooden[13] the inner ear arrangement of echidnas provides an ideal pathway to pick up ground vibrations which would assist in finding food.

We have observed how echidnas incorporate acute hearing with learning and intelligence. Each radio transmitter placed on an echidna has a different frequency with slightly different pulse rates and pitches. Although we attempt to keep the receiver volume as low as possible when radio tracking, it is inevitable that animals sometimes hear their own frequency. Suspecting that animals recognised transmitter sounds, we designed and conducted a series of experiments. Not only do echidnas learn to distinguish the sound of their transmitter from others, it only takes them a day or two to learn this. Even when the bush is full of bird calls, echidnas can sort out the sound of the receiver from the noisy surroundings. Some animals bolt for cover when they hear their own frequency or start digging in. If another frequency is tuned in, echidnas remain silent and motionless until the tracker has passed.

To avoid echidnas hearing the receiver, we have tried using earphones. After frustrations of getting tangled in dense vegetation, this was abandoned. Another problem of tracking in many habitats, with or without headphones, is walking quietly. It takes a lot of practice and skill to be able to follow an echidna unobtrusively.

Eyes

In 1979 animal psychologist Richard Gates wrote, "Flat corneas and protruding eyes probably give the echidna a panoramic view of the world...[14]" Despite the facts, it is not unusual to hear that some

The skull of the short-beaked echidna is more reminiscent of a bird than a mammal. The beak is part of the skull structure. The cranium protects a complex brain with large neocortex, the site of complex mental functions.

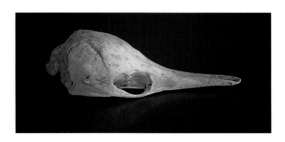

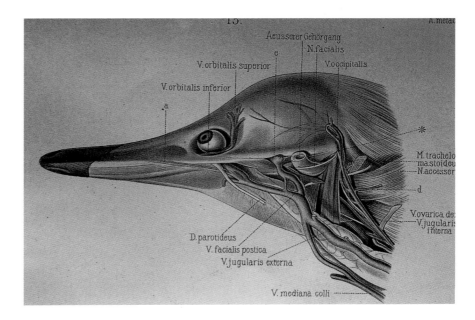

people believe echidnas are blind. Although eyesight is not the echidna's most acute sense, they recognise movements, shapes, sizes, orientation and tones. Echidnas have no colour vision, as cones are absent. The eye is a pure rod retinal system. Gates showed that echidnas could discriminate between black and white, vertical and horizontal strips at different angles, widths and distances. He concluded that echidnas use eyesight and can learn to use visual cues. Looking at the skull, the echidna's eyes are large, but appear outwardly small. They are protected by eyelids and have relatively long eyelashes to afford ease of cleaning after digging activities.

BEAK

The name short-beaked echidna refers to the bony protrusion which is part of the skull structure. The skull is more reminiscent of a bird than a mammal. The long-beaked echidna of New Guinea has the same bony protrusion, but its beak is nearly twice as long! Tough, soft skin covers the echidna's beak. The nostrils are located on top and near the apex. Unlike the platypus, which closes its nostrils with a flap of skin when it goes under water for food, the nostrils of the echidna always stay open. Why don't they get clogged with dirt, sand and soil as the echidna digs for its food? You don't have to be standing very far from a foraging echidna to hear the snorts it emits. They blow short puffs of air through their nostrils to keep them clean. Echidnas produce a fair amount of mucus for clearing the air passage, so much in fact that I have seen them blowing bubbles out of their nostrils. The delicate looking beak is powerful enough to pry bark off trees and flip rocks. The physics and mechanics behind the beak strength is the double wedge shape[15]. However, if an echidna damages the end of its beak it can be fatal as it can no longer take in food or breathe properly. In 85% of all road kills examined over the years, death has occurred due to beak damage.

Mouth and Tongue

On the underside of the beak is the echidna's small mouth opening which has a gape of about 5 mm (1/4 in). There are no conspicuous lips. The lower jaws of most mammals are articulated allowing the mouth to open and close for chewing, vocalising or carrying things. The two long narrow jaw bones of the echidna are not efficiently hinged, but rotate about their own long axes to open and close the mouth.

When they find food, the echidna's worm-like tongue, measuring up to 17 cm (7 in) flicks out. Rapid in-and-out darting action is controlled by two large muscles extending to the back of the throat. The surface of the tongue is covered with rows of barblike structures. Copious amounts of saliva secreted by glands in the throat make the tongue sticky to the touch. Using the mucus secretion and barbs, the echidna tongue draws prey into the mouth. Echidnas have no teeth for chewing. The palate on the roof of the echidnas mouth has rows of spines made of a horny substance. Food is ground to a fine paste-like consistency between the rough pad on back of the tongue and the top of the mouth before swallowing.

Stomach and Digestion

Digestion in echidnas is slow. Unlike other mammals the lining of the stomach is unusual because it contains no secretory glands to aid digestion. The stomach consists of a rough horny skin. Through peristaltic movement the stomach grinds dirt and food, helping to break

There are blond, brunette and redhead echidnas in the Kangaroo Island population. The soft body fur is often mottled or shows distinct patterns which can change over an individual's lifespan. Mainland echidnas are generally uniformly dark.

down hard insect exoskeletons. Digestion takes place primarily in the 3.4 metre-long (11 ft) small intestine. In one experiment, zoologist Mervyn Griffiths fed a captive echidna one species of termite and used another as a marker. The marker species was not seen in the excrement until two full days later. New born humans weigh about the same as an adult echidna. Their small intestine is about the same length too. However, the time it takes food to pass through the human digestive tract is only four to six hours.

FEET AND CLAWS

Roots snap and rubble flies when an echidna starts digging. The front legs and shoulders are built like powerful earth moving equipment. Echidnas can dig under large rocks, too heavy for average humans to lift, and pop them loose from the ground. This allows space for the agile tongue to search for food. An engineer equated this feat with a human supporting a compact car on his shoulders while another person changed the tyre! Echidnas execute feats of strength through the physics of their unique anatomy. Arrangement of the shoulder girdle and pelvis along with their remarkable system of muscle insertion are well engineered to transfer loads[16]. These mechanical advantages increase the echidna's muscle power several fold. Sometimes the spines are incorporated into this unique lifting and moving system.

Both front and back feet of an echidna have five digits. Shaped like garden spades, the front claws are longest in the middle, bordered by short ones on either side. The first claw on the hind foot is small and thumblike. The elongated second claw, known as the grooming claw, is usually curved. Because of femur and pelvis construction, the echidna can use the grooming claw on almost any region of the body to rid itself of a parasite or just to have a good scratch. The remaining three claws can be of varying length depending on where the echidna lives, i.e. to which subspecies it belongs. Unlike other mammals, the echidna is capable of digging straight down. Using front and hind feet in a circular manner, it disappears in a matter of minutes leaving only a mound of churned up dirt.

An echidna's pelvic girdle is typically mammalian, but the bones of the hind limbs are short and stout. Because the bones in the lower part of the leg (tibia and fibula) are rotated compared to their position in other mammals, the hind feet turn outward and point backwards.

An echidna beak is covered with soft skin. Numerous nerves and blood vessels surround the nostrils, located on the top of the beak, near the tip. On the underside, the tiny mouth opens only as wide as the width of the tongue.

(Above) How an echidna mouth works is best seen in a dissection. Food sticks to fine barbs on the tongue surface. The base of the tongue has a horny plate where food is ground against the ridged palate. An adult echidna tongue can extend up to 17 cm (7 in) out of the mouth.

(Right) The echidna's sensitive eyes are well-protected from loose soil and debris as the beak pushes and probes dirt and plant litter, flips stones and breaks away bark. Dirt is cleared from the nostrils with frequent snorts and bubbles of mucus.

There is a fleshy bump on the inside of the hind ankle of all echidnas, which may or may not contain a spur. In adult platypuses, spurs are only found on males. These are connected to a venom gland[17]. Spurs of echidnas are not connected to a venom gland and no one knows for sure why they are present.

The echidna's digging abilities and strength are legendary. We often find animals by hearing their tenacious digging. When brought into captivity, they have been known to dig through wooden garage doors, plastic garbage bins and even old refrigerators.

POUCH

An echidna's pouch is different from that of a kangaroo and many other marsupials. It is not a permanent "pocket," and is only fully developed by females who are preparing to lay an egg and suckle a young. At this stage the mammary glands swell and form the fleshy lips of the pouch along the lateral muscles of the stomach. These muscles support the egg during incubation and later the young in the pouch. Since the echidna walks on all fours, the pouch on the belly opens downward, towards the ground. Males, females and juveniles all have the ability to pull stomach muscles together to give a pouch-like appearance.

Echidnas can lower body temperature and metabolism in order to save energy. This is called torpor. Kangaroo Island echidnas use torpor at any time of the year, for example when it is hot during the summer and food is less available. When and how long echidnas go torpid is an individual trait.

Echidnas have no teats or nipples. On the belly, approximately where the teats would be, are two small, circular, hairy areas. Each area or areola consists of approximately 120 pores and is present in both males and females. In females the areolas are called milk patches. A specialised mammary hair protrudes from every pore[18]. During lactation, milk is excreted and suckled by the young from the milk patch.

Scrutinising the belly side of an echidna reveals another mammalian anomaly: there are no obvious clues to the gender of the animal. There is only the one hole, the cloaca, through which faecal, urinary and reproductive products are excreted. All genitals are located internally. The male's testes are positioned high inside the body, at about the level of the kidneys. The penis, an intriguing bifid organ with four openings that vaguely resembles a small cauliflower, lays in a ventral sac inside the cloaca. It is not used for urination and is only outside of the body during mating. Vive la difference!

BODY TEMPERATURE AND TORPOR

Another astonishing echidna fact is its low body temperature. Since 1879 when Brisbane based biologist Nicoli Miklouho-Maclay[19] recorded an astonishing cloaca temperature of 28.3°C (82.9°F) in an active echidna, scientists have investigated this phenomenon. Most mammals function at a body temperature close to 37°C (98.6°F). Mean active body temperature of an echidna is between 31 and 33°C (87.8 - 91.4°F)! Although excellent at coping with low temperatures, echidnas cannot tolerate temperatures greater than 35°C (95°F) for any length of time. If an echidna's body temperature reaches that of a human (37°C or 98.6°F), it will die of heat stress. One unexplored area concerning the spines is their possible role in regulating body temperature. Echidnas do not tolerate high temperatures well. Field observations indicate that the spines and the highly vascularised muscle the root goes into help dissipate heat from the body. Echidnas have no sweat pores to help keep cool nor do they pant.

Some animals can lower their body temperature and metabolism to save energy. This is called torpor. Miklouho-Maclay speculated that echidnas went torpid. In 1989[20] scientists actually documented torpor

(Right) The hind foot has 5 claws and sometimes a spur. The small thumb is often obscured by fur. The long second claw is referred to as the grooming claw. It is used like an agile finger to remove parasites or have a good scratch.

(Below) Echidna feet are digging machines. Massive claws coupled with the extraordinary ability to dig straight down enable them to move vertically through dirt. The front foot has 5 spade-shaped claws. The foot is a mass of muscle and tendons capable of snapping roots and breaking hard pan soil.

in a wild, free-living population. Echidnas living above the snow line in the Australian Alps dropped their body temperature as low as 4°C (39.2°F). Tasmanian researchers[21] determined that respiration rates of torpid echidnas varied between 1breath/min. to 1 breath/3 min. They also measured periods of apnea, when an animal did not breath, lasting up to two hours.

In the temperate climatic region of Kangaroo Island, we have found that all echidnas can use torpor, but duration is individualistic[22]. In our study site, torpor is not restricted to the winter months, but may occur at any time of the year. During the heat of the summer, some echidnas bury themselves or find a cool cave where they remain inactive for one or more days with body temperatures just above ground temperature. Echidnas were once thought of as primitive mammals with inferior and incomplete ability to regulate their body temperature. Having a low and variable body temperature may have enhanced echidna survival through the ages. Scientists now realise torpor is a sophisticated physiological process.

(Above) Echidnas are masters of camouflage. At a distance, their colour and shape allow them to blend in and disappear. Even in open country they may look like a rock or bush in native vegetation.

(Opposite) Monotremes have been erroneously considered "primitive" mammals because of their many physical differences. Reproducing by laying an egg, having a low, variable body temperature and feeding on invertebrates may be significant to their long survival.

IN THE BUSH

(Above) Gary Larson must have been thinking about echidnas when he drew this cartoon. No one knows for certain why the dinosaurs became extinct, nor do we know all of the secrets of monotreme survival.

(Opposite) The echidna's success is due to many factors, including not overpopulating and not competing among themselves for food and shelter.

T ERRIBLE LIZARD

Dinosaur. It's a word that awakens the imagination and conjures up images of primeval times and awesome animals. Everyone knows something about dinosaurs, but few have an inkling about the curious creatures that roamed the planet at the same time. They were ancestors to our modern day echidna. As coincidence would have it one man researched both, but their coexistence on earth would not be discovered in his life time.

British anatomist Sir Richard Owen, a founder of the British Natural History Museum, not only coined the term *Dinosaur*, but he also spent a good deal of time looking at monotreme specimens (both echidnas and platypuses) sent from Australia to England. By 1834 Owen believed that as much as possible had been learned from dead specimens. He published a series of questions that he felt could only be answered by direct observation of the animals in the field. Thirty-one years later, in 1865, he restated his questions about monotremes, as none of them had been answered, or even addressed. In 1881 George Bennett Jr., a British naturalist working in Australia, added yet another question to be resolved. At this time, scientists still believed that monotremes gave birth to live young. The unanswered questions were:

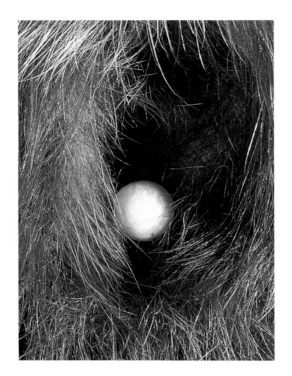

1) How do monotremes mate?
2) What is the length of gestation, the period between mating and egg-laying?
3) How does a foetus breath and how is it nourished?
4) What is the size, condition and power of the young at the time of birth?
5) How long does the young suckle (length of lactation)?
6) At what age does the animal attain its full size (become sexually mature)?
7) When do monotremes mate?
8) How often does a sexually mature female reproduce?

EGG EXTRAORDINAIRE

Echidna Time. New discoveries do not happen quickly. Ninety-two years after the first European description of the echidna came a great revelation—echidnas are egg-laying mammals! The year 1884 was a monumental monotreme year. Egg-laying was discovered in both echidnas and platypuses. Miraculously, two different people in different parts of Australia simultaneously uncovered this monotreme reproductive sensation.

(Above) Although the echidna pouch opens towards the ground and does not form a deep pocket like marsupials, the female can forage and remain active throughout incubation. The egg is moved from side to side in the furry pouch.

(Right) An echidna egg is about the same diameter as an Australian five-cent coin or an American dime. The shell is soft and rubbery, like some reptile eggs; it has the texture of a firm green grape.

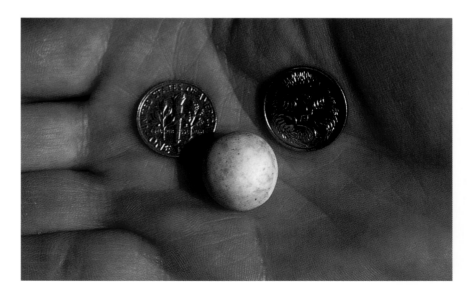

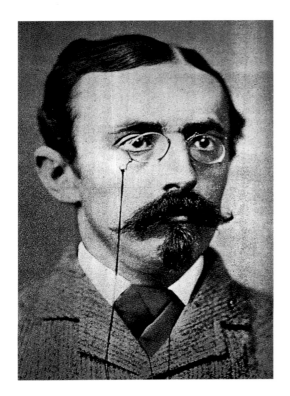

Dr. Wihelm Haacke was acting director of the South Australian Museum in 1884 when he discovered an egg in the pouch of an echidna. It had taken science over 90 years to discover that monotremes were egg-laying mammals.

William Caldwell[1] from the University of Cambridge, England arrived in Australia in September 1883 to study the development of Australian mammals. He worked in the Burnett district of Queensland where both echidnas and platypuses "seemed to be very numerous." During the third week of August, 1884 he found an egg in the pouch of an echidna. According to his report, he then shot a platypus with one egg laid and the second in a "dilated *os uteri.*" This infers that he actually shot the platypus in its burrow, as platypuses do not form a pouch, but incubate their eggs between their tail and body. How Caldwell accomplished this we will never know.

On 29 August, 1884 Caldwell sent the following telegram to the British Association in Montreal: *Monotremes oviparous, ovum meroblastic,* which translates to "Monotremes lay eggs, the ovum or egg germ cell undergoes only partial division as in bird and reptile development."

At the same time some 1,600 km away in South Australia, Dr. William Haacke[2], acting director for the South Australian Museum in Adelaide was examining two echidnas that were taken on Kangaroo Island at the beginning of August "in copulation." On 25 August 1884, Haacke examined the pouch of the female in hopes of finding a newly born young. When the female was unrolled, he did not find a young echidna, but discovered an egg. Haacke was so excited by the smooth, leathery soft-shelled egg that he accidentally squished it between his fingers!

It doesn't really matter whether Haacke or Caldwell was the first to scientifically document egg-laying in monotremes. The fact remains, it took 92 years to find out that echidnas were egg-laying mammals. A long time in human history, but only a minuscule period when related to 120 million years of adaptation.

Discovery of egg-laying mammals promoted a renaissance of field work in Australia. By the turn of the century, light had been shed on two of the eight echidna reproductive mysteries. Early anatomical discoveries by Sir Richard Owen and field observations by British

Dr. Richard Semon of Germany led a scientific expedition to Australia between 1891 and 1893. His major goals were to learn more about the reproductive biology of the echidna and the lungfish. His work represents a body of field knowledge that would not be possible to collect today.

naturalist George Bennett Jr. suggested that echidnas bred during the winter months. This was verified by German field researcher, Richard Semon in 1891[3]. Another researcher suggested that echidna gestation could be as short as 18 days or as long as 28 days[4]. With the discovery of egg-laying, other new questions arose. One was: How long do echidnas incubate the egg before it hatches?

MONOTREME MERV

During the 1950s Dr. Mervyn Griffiths, a Canberra based CSIRO (Commonwealth Science and Industry Research Organisation) scientist, became interested in echidnas and platypuses. Over the next four decades his research either answered or supplied the first factual information for questions posed between 1835 and 1900. Griffiths verified that echidnas throughout Australia breed during the winter. He discovered that an echidna incubates its egg for 10.5 days before hatching. He was the first person to weigh and measure a hatchling echidna, monitor growth of the young and estimate length of lactation. Griffiths documented that young echidnas suckle, not lick, the milk at the milk patch and he was the first to experimentally show in the field that females suckle burrow young in intervals of five or more days. Other aspects of Griffiths work include physiology, embryology, morphology, histology, biochemistry, genetics and phylogeny of both echidnas and platypuses. In depth echidna information about Griffiths own work and that of many other monotreme researchers can be found in his books *Echidnas* and *Biology of the Monotremes*.

Merv has been a mentor for most monotreme researchers. Always available with an open ear and helpful suggestions, he quieted one of my early concerns about the possibility of a female refusing her young after handling. In his typical relaxed manner he replied, "We don't even know how often the female reproduces, she must be maternal!" He was right. Thanks, Merv.

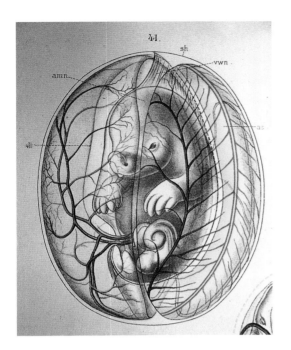

One of Semon's illustrations shows an echidna embryo in the egg. During the 10.5-day incubation period, the young develop an enamel-covered egg tooth. This is used to help rupture the soft eggshell at hatching and is then shed.

COURTSHIP

During most of the year echidnas lead a solitary life style, never directly interacting with other echidnas in the area. Prior to breeding, things change. At this time of year you might luck out and find two, three or even six animals together, an echidna train. Echidna trains occur from the beginning of courtship through breeding. Trains have been sighted as early as April and as late as October, but June to August, winter in Australia, is prime echidna train time. Trains of three to four animals are common, but up to ten have been reported in recent years . The largest group of echidnas ever recorded on Kangaroo Island was by a fisherman whose ship went aground in 1838. After sheltering for the night in an old homestead he wrote in his journal: "When we emerged at daylight, 25 porcupines, with bristles up, were nestled near the doorway and we nearly stepped on them. This ended our first shipwrecked night.[5]" All trains have one thing in common: there is only one female. She is generally the largest and in the lead[6]. We often get reports of people seeing an echidna family out walking. The largest animal, suspected to be the father is in front, followed by a somewhat smaller individual and a 'baby' bringing up the rear. In reality the "family" is a courtship train[7]. How a female's size relates to the size of the males pursuing her is unknown. On Kangaroo Island we have recorded larger males forming trains with larger females whereas smaller males were lured by smaller females[8]. How do they find each other? Our field work has given us some answers.

I was out searching with a volunteer on a cool, rainy day in mid-July when we spotted five echidnas out foraging. While gawking at this astonishing sight, our presence was felt and the animals split into five different directions. I ran after the largest one, hoping it was the female and the others disappeared into the bush. Feeling silly for losing four echidnas, we secured the one animal in a hessian bag and began to search. We returned an hour later empty-handed to find two echidnas poking and sniffing around the bag. These were bagged and we returned to base camp. The first echidna was a female and the two caught sniffing around the bag were males. This

Drs. Mervyn Griffiths (left), Peggy Rismiller and Michael Messer (right) collect milk samples from Kangaroo Island echidnas. These samples provided more information about milk composition and were used to research the divergence time of monotreme lineage.

raised questions. How did the males know where the female was, scent or sound?

We attached radiotransmitters to the males and returned them immediately to their place of capture. We transmitted the female, but retained her overnight in a hessian bag. The next day she was released and the empty bag was put out as a "lure." Within three hours two males came to sniff and prod at the empty bag. This experiment was repeated at different times of the year and in different locations. Males are only attracted to a bag that has contained a sexually active female during the breeding season. This indicates that males are responding to a pheromone.

As yet, no one has discovered the source of this pheromone. During the courtship period we have observed males sniffing the footsteps of females as they wander off. The spur pocket on the inside of the hind feet sometimes contains a waxy substance which may be the origin of the attractant. In male platypuses, spur secretion increases during the breeding season and correlates with levels of testosterone[9]. No one has examined the spur secretion of either male or female echidnas. Whatever attracts a male, he may travel well outside of his normal home range in search of a mate.

Courtship lasts from one to six weeks and different males may join or drop out of the train. During this time animals are often oblivious to their surroundings. They have been spotted by bushwalkers in woodlands, by drivers crossing roads, by surfers on the beach, by farmers in the barn and even gathered around the tyre of a parked car! Typical male courtship behaviour includes nudging or sniffing around the female and trying to be first in line behind her when she moves off into the bush. Males must remain persistent and patient, because until the female is receptive, they have no chance of mating. Mating can occur at any time of the day or night in many types of locations.

MATING RITES IN A RUT

Since 1834 Europeans have wondered how monotremes mate. Surely
the indigenous Australian people knew. I often wonder why the
information was not shared. Perhaps Aboriginals were not asked or it
was simply something that was not talked about. When I started
working with echidnas in 1988, observations of how echidnas mate in
the wild were not documented. By radio-tracking echidnas day and
night during the rainy, winter breeding season, I finally ended up at

(Opposite) Echidna trains, one female followed by one or more males, are seen only during the winter breeding season. In our study population females generally mated once every 3 to 5 years while males could be sexually active every year.

(Below) How do males find a female during the breeding season? We now know that females produce a pheromone that attracts the males up to the time of mating. There may be other behavioural or physiological enticements that have not yet been discovered.

the right place, at the right time. Sitting quiet and soaked on a slippery hill side, I peered through the bushes and watched the ritual.

There were five echidnas gathered around the base of a small tree with low-hanging branches. Blondie, a light-colored female, lay flat on her stomach with front claws anchored at the base of the tree. Two males dug on either side of her body, as the others attempted to secure positions beside her. The males pushed and dug, forming a circular trench around Blondie and the tree. When the mating rut was about 15 cm (6 in) deep, one male, Puncture, turned and challenged one of his competitor's. Heads butted against each other in a reverse tug-of-war. They pushed each other to and fro until the competitor was shoved out of the mating rut and disappeared into the bush. Puncture continued challenging until he was the only remaining male. During this entire time Blondie had not moved, but continued to lay outstretched on the ground. Puncture continued digging on one side of Blondie, attempting to lift her tail with his hind leg. Occasionally he would stop digging and run his front paw from head to tail over her spines, which undulated with the stroking motion. Once Blondie's tail had been lifted enough for Puncture to place his tail under hers, he lay on his side in the trench hardly moving.

(Above) Echidna home ranges naturally encompass areas of human habitation. During the breeding season trains have been spotted in the most unlikely places, including clustered about this tyre of a parked car.

(Below) Field observations record many instances of adaptability. This male is holding onto the female's tracking transmitter during mating. He would usually dig a trench beside her to avoid rolling on his back during the cloaca-on-cloaca copulation.

Mating took place cloaca on cloaca. After remaining coupled for over an hour, they separated and the male wandered off. The mating ritual and the rain had lasted nearly five hours.

Sometimes there is only a single male with the female when she is receptive. In this case he digs on only one side of her body until he can lift and place his tail under hers in the mating position. In the more than 20 echidna matings we have observed, copulation lasted between 30 and 180 minutes. In every incidence, the female bred with just one male. Within 48 hours of mating, the female is back to a solitary lifestyle. Pheromones and other attractants seem to "turn off." Males either return to their own home ranges or go in search of another female. After a decade of observing echidna courtship and mating, it is still a mystery as to which male will be the chosen breeder.

A deep trench, or mating rut, is usually left around the female after breeding. Pheromones and other attractants seem to be turned off at this point and the female goes back to her solitary lifestyle. Males may continue to court other females. During the breeding season a male can lose up to 25% of his body mass.

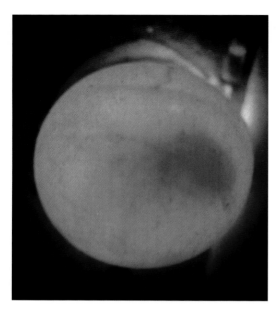

Candling an echidna egg at day 6 during incubation reveals the developing puggle filling about one third of the entire egg. Blood vessels connecting the young to the nurturing yolk sac are clearly visible.

BACHELOR PARTY

While the female prepares to lay an egg, what are male echidnas doing? Early in my echidna field work, I discovered a behaviour that still baffles me. It was September 1992, post breeding season. I had radio tracked Kikko to a small thicket of dead prickly acacia. All of a sudden my receiver was going click, pop, thud, click, pop thud in an erratic rhythm. This meant that other signals were interfering with the one I was tracking. Checking frequencies, I identified the signals of two other males, Casey and Popcorn. They were in same bush with Kikko. My logical deduction: a late train and an unknown female without a transmitter!

Peering under the dead prickly plant I could not see a spine or a movement. I gingerly pushed my hands into the soft soil, located the back of an echidna and felt the transmitter. Not the one I wanted. Moving methodically around the base of the bush two more echidnas were located by touch, both having transmitters. "Female must be buried deeper between the males" I thought. My next move? Remove the males. After Popcorn, Casey and Kikko had been unearthed, there was still no female to be found. Bewildered and a bit frustrated, I pulled out the dead bush. On hands and knees I excavated and felt the soil in a metre radius around where the males had been peacefully resting. No female. Looking around, embarrassed at my overzealous digging, I recorded the observations in my book: three males together, no female. While scooping the soil back into place, I was reminded of keeping an open mind when working with echidnas.

When I found "males only" together in the following year after breeding I was not so surprised. It is, in fact, a regular occurrence here, and recently colleagues in Tasmania observed it as well. We may never know the reason for this phenomena, but I have my own theory. It is a bachelor party commiserating the post-breeding blues. We hope to get a better understanding of this behaviour when we can unintrusively monitor hormone levels.

THEN CAME AN EGG

At the turn of the century, German researcher Richard Semon[10] painstakingly documented growth of echidna embryos with detailed illustrations that have yet to be surpassed. Oogenesis, how egg and embryo develop during gestation, was studied extensively in echidnas between 1930 and 1990[11,12,13,14,15]. Accurate verification of the gestation period has taken longer. In 1989 Mervyn Griffiths wrote: "Information on the gestation period in *Tachyglossus* is sketchy." Up to this time most echidna literature deduced that gestation was "about three weeks." Since 1990 we have observed more than 20 matings and documented nearly 30 incidences of egg-laying and hatching. Each time there was no egg in the pouch on day 21, but when checked on days 22 to 24 after mating, an egg was found. From this we conclude that echidna gestation is 23 days with individual variations of 12 hours either way.

A female echidna lays a single egg directly into her pouch, but until recently no one had actually observed this act. Early naturalists speculated that the egg was rolled into the pouch with her beak. Given the location of the pouch and the shape of the animal, this was not a satisfying explanation. In more recent years scientists have observed cloacal extrusion. They speculated that it could be extended to the pouch opening and the egg placed inside.

We have observed echidnas in a sitting position when they were grooming either themselves or their pouch young. Because this is a vulnerable position and echidnas are difficult to approach without disturbing them, very few people have seen this. Once, while observing a sitting female, I didn't know whether to trust my eyes. When she unrolled and walked off, we retrieved her and found what I thought I observed happening. There was an egg in the pouch! Another mystery solved! The female does curl up in a sitting position to safely deposit a single egg into her pouch.

When an egg was found in the pouch of an echidna in 1884, the researcher was so surprised that he accidentally ruptured the soft shell while examining it. Up to that time, people believed that echidnas gave birth to live young.

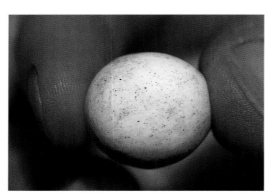

When the egg is first laid it is white, nearly round and between 14 and 16 mm (about 5/8 in.) in diameter, slightly smaller than an Australian five-cent coin or about the size an American dime. The shell of the egg is soft and leathery. Its texture and consistency is like a small, firm green grape. We've documented that the female actually moves the egg from one side of the pouch to the other, but it is not known if this movement is important for the development of the embryo. During incubation in the pouch, cells in the egg multiply and the young takes on a beanlike shape. The embryo grows a minute enamel-covered egg tooth to assist in hatching. As the days pass dirt and moisture in the pouch give the egg an earthy patina. Just prior to hatching, the egg becomes elongated. Maybe this is caused by the young moving inside the egg. The egg is in the pouch, but where is the mother during this incubation period?

MOVIN' MAMA

One of my jobs as a post doctoral student was to help find echidnas with an egg in the pouch. There was next to nothing written about the female's behaviour at egg-laying, so I asked the advise of experi-

It is unusual to see an echidna sitting on its tail. In this position, the female extends her muscular cloaca and deposits the soft-shelled egg directly into the pouch. She also sits this way to clean the pouch young.

Contrary to popular belief, many female echidnas actively forage and move with an egg in their pouch. It was once believed that the female went into a burrow to lay her single egg and that she did not emerge until the young hatched.

enced echidna researchers. Although no one had conclusive evidence, the theory was that the female entered an "incubation burrow," laid her egg and remained there for the entire 10.5-day incubation period. Reasoning behind this was that the pouch was fairly superficial. After the egg hatched and the young was clinging to the hairs in the pouch, the female could safely leave the burrow.

Armed with this information, we put radio transmitters on as many females as possible during the breeding season. When they remained underground for more than two days, we retrieved them to check their pouch. Sometimes an egg was found, sometimes not. Females who remained active, were not pouch-checked as we believed they could not have an egg. As the season drew to a close and all volunteers left, Mike and I remained to retrieve transmitters from the field. On our last planned field day we went to retrieve a transmitter from a female who was seen actively foraging everyday around noon. Before removing the transmitter, we decided to check the pouch—just in case—I had become quite adept at cautiously probing the pouch with a finger to feel for an egg. When her pouch felt different, warm and moist instead of dry and cool, Mike could tell by the expression on my face we had something. Carefully unrolling her we opened the pouch to find a young just hatching out of an egg! How many other echidnas had been running around with an egg in their

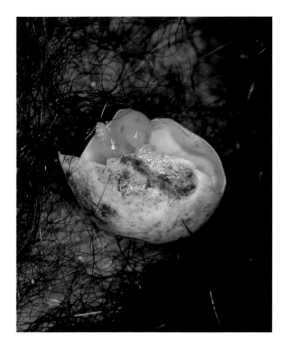

After 10.5 days incubation in the pouch, the minute puggle hatches from the egg. It took many years of studying reproductive and maternal behaviour in the wild before we developed unintrusive methods of observing events such as egg laying and hatching.

pouch and we had simply not looked! We came very close to falling into the trap expounded by evolutionist Geoffroy Saint-Hilaire: Scientific theory has the extraordinary power of hindering the discovery of fact!

Over the years we have learned that some females do in fact dig an incubation burrow and remain there until the egg hatches. Others lay the egg and continue normal daily activities. We've even observed females with an egg travelling through water or traversing a swamp as part of their daily movements. What determines the different behaviour is unknown. Perhaps it has to do with age and experience or it may simply be individual variation.

DAY 10.5

A clear liquid surrounds the embryo that has been developing for ten and a half days within the egg. Somehow, the minute egg tooth catches hold of the leathery shell and begins splitting it open. Assisted by the moisture that pours from the egg into the pouch, the baby echidna, known as a puggle, wiggles its way out.

Seeing this remarkable event is an experience beyond words. Each time I find I hold my breath as the tiny, pinkish blob with minute limbs and transparent claws grabs for a single hair in the pouch and pulls itself forward. Its size is less than half the volume of the egg, only about the length of my little finger nail, and it weighs about one third of a gram (300 mg). One Australian five-cent coin or American dime weighs as much as seven to eight newly hatched echidnas.

Blood vessels show bright red through the translucent body contrasted by the dark bands of inner organs. There are tiny dark spots under the skin where the eyes will appear. While the front limbs are well developed to grasp for the hairs in the pouch (its lifehold), hind limbs are mere formless buds. Nature is miraculous. In six months this vulnerable, slippery mass of cells will be a well-spined echidna!

72

It takes 7 to 8 newly hatched echidnas to weigh as much as an Australian five-cent coin or an American dime. At hatching it grasps the hairs of the mother's pouch and pulls itself 6 to 7 times it body length to the milk patch where it suckles.

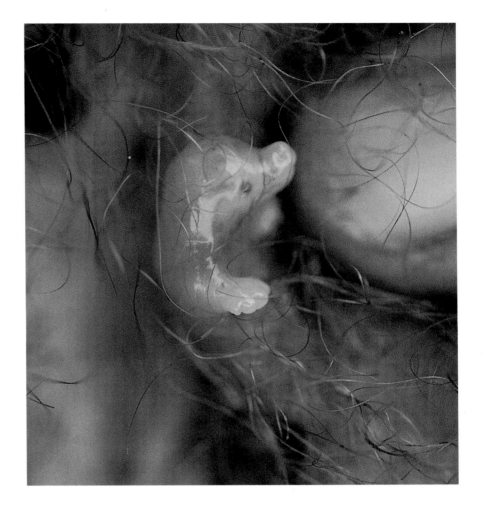

MONOTREME MOMENTS

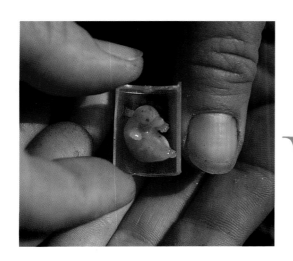

(Above) A tiny plastic container is used to weigh and measure this newly hatched puggle. This procedure protects its sensitive, translucent skin. Data is collected and the puggle returned to the pouch in less than 60 seconds.

(Opposite) Burrow young echidnas are nursed by their mothers only once every 5 days. They suckle large amounts of milk taking in up to 40% of their own body mass, then sleep, digest and wait for the mother to return.

W HAT DO YOU CALL A BABY ECHIDNA? In the winter of 1988, Earthwatch volunteers from Australia, Great Britain and the United Stated were helping with echidna research when a female echidna carrying a pouch young was brought in. "What do you call a baby echidna?" asked one volunteer. Everyone looked to the Australians. "Well, a 'joey' is the young of a marsupial, but I don't know the name for a baby echidna," answered one. "It's so strange and... uh... organic, it must have a name," injected an American volunteer. "How about calling it a pug?" suggested our English teacher volunteer. "Pug is a term for an imp or dwarf animal and it also means a piece of clay."

Several days later Mike joined us and brought in an echidna. As we uncurled her, the egg was hatching. All volunteers watched in stunned silence as a beanlike squirming blob emerged from the soft, leathery egg. "WOW," whispered someone. "That is tiny!" "A puggle," murmured the school teacher. After mother and young were returned to the bush, discussion ensued about finding a new word and a name for a baby echidna.

"Wait a minute," Mike piped up, "the word 'puggle' has been around for a long time. Its origin goes back to 17th-century English[1] and it has been used both as a noun and a verb. While I was working with

Fingers gently part the pouch folds to reveal a minute puggle. It turns towards the sudden light invading its normally dark home. Milk visible in the stomach indicates that it has just suckled.

an old rabbiter in the early 1970s he told me about 'puggles.' The word came from the practice of bush people 'puggling' a hole in search of rabbits and occasionally turning up this strange baby animal." We documented this and the name was introduced into scientific literature.

IN THE POUCH

The egg hatches in the snug little pocket at the bottom, the posterior end of the pouch. Clinging to its mother's belly hairs, the puggle's first movement is towards the source of food, the milk patches. The distance covered for this journey represents six times its own body length. Scent probably directs it to the milk patch, but this behaviour needs more investigation. The puggle is so minute that the belly hairs hardly move as it grasps, pulls and wiggles to its destination. At the areolas, or milk patches, the translucent puggle suckles, not licks the milk from the base of the mammary hairs[2].

Weighing and measuring my first 24-hour-old puggle was a bit scary. I called Merv, the only person I knew who had weighed a hatchling before me. His advice was, "Work very carefully." Thinking laterally, we cut a small specimen container in half, unrolled the female and gently scooped up the squirming puggle. It weighed 0.289 g. A string was used to measure its length from snout tip to tail tip. Its tiny curved body was 23 mm (7/8 in) long. In less than a minute the puggle was returned to the moist safety of the pouch. We also discovered that the egg shell was no longer in the pouch. No one has ever observed the mother removing the shell, but I surmise that she must help dislodge it from the moist, sticky hairs. Perhaps the shell presents a hindrance for the tiny baby and is therefore removed.

The puggle leads an extraordinary life, clinging blind, spineless and upside down to its mother's belly. Mum travels and forages on her four short legs moving with a rolling gait or waving waddle. Her superficial pouch gapes open to the earth and the fleshy lips do not form a tight closure. However, the young does not fall out or drown while suckling in this upside down position. You can actually hear the

76

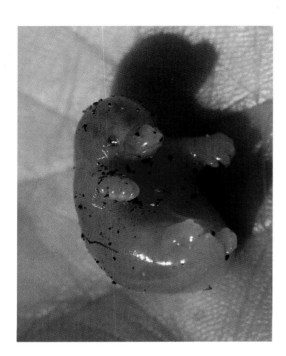

(Above) From 0.3 to 1.0 grams in 2 days! At hatching, the hind legs are nearly invisible buds. At 2 days of age they are distinct and the young has more than tripled its body mass.

(Right) At 11 days of age the pigmentation in the beak becomes apparent. It now weighs 9.1 grams. The skin is still shiny from moisture in the mother's pouch. No one knows for sure if the moisture is to protect the sensitive skin or aid in building immune defences.

(Below) After being removed from the pouch for weighing and measuring, this 14-day-old puggle instinctively grabs for the hairs on the mother's belly and turns itself upside down.

(Opposite, top left) At 22 days of age the young is a 52-gram ball of pink wiggling muscle. We don't know how much it moves while in the pouch, but when removed for measurements it never stops twisting and turning.

(Opposite, below) Soft fuzz-like hair begins to appear at 34 days. The muscles that form the pouch are clearly discernible, as are the grooming claws on the hind feet.

(Opposite, top right). When about 45 days old, dark spine stubbles erupt, causing the skin colour to turn from pink to grey.

puggle slurping at the milk patch without disturbing the mother. How often it actually suckles in early life is unknown, but it grows rapidly. After just a couple of days the obscure buds on its hind legs sprout well-formed feet and the grooming claws become discernible. We have found the humidity in the pouch remains above 90% for up to 14 days after hatching. During this time the puggle increases its body mass over 100-fold, from less than a third of a gram to over 30 grams! Imagine newborn human babies, who weigh as much as an adult echidna (3 kg or 6.5 lbs) growing at that rate. They would weigh 300 kg (650 lbs) after only two weeks. Echidna milk, which is high in fat[3], protein[4] and iron[5,6], changes in colour and composition as the puggle continues to grow. Soon its skin toughens and is no longer translucent. At this stage the mother's pouch becomes a dry nest.

One of my most vivid memories of removing a large puggle from the pouch was the smell. Focused on my work, I did not take time to analyse the odour on my hands until the puggle was safely back in the pouch. Wrinkling my nose at the faint but pungent perfume, my mind wandered back to my childhood in Ohio. Closing my eyes and smelling again, the origin of the smell popped into my mind, a skunk. Throughout life in the pouch this distinct, but subdued scent clings to the young and anyone who touches it. Perhaps it has to do with mother/young recognition or is simply caused by excrement.

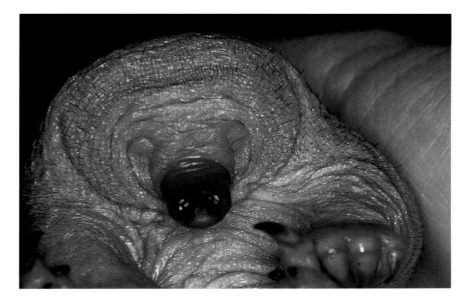

Whatever the origin, once the puggle leaves the pouch for good, its odorous aura vanishes.

When the puggle is between 30 and 40 days old, light coloured fuzz appears on the skin surface. Soon the pink skin turns to grey as coarser hairs and spines erupt. Because the baby no longer fits in the pouch, the mother is forced to walk on tippy-toes as the growing puggle clings to the belly hairs, sometimes scraping the ground. More than one puggle have been found dead on an *Iridomyrmex* nest, a common meat-eating ant in the Australian bush. They probably lost their grip when biting ants swarmed the mother as she traversed the area. This is the time for the female to place her young in the safety of a nursery burrow. At 50 to 60 days of age, the life of the puggle changes dramatically.

BURROW LIFE

A nursery burrow, like an echidna shelter site, can be almost anywhere. A female will expand a natural space, such as in tree roots and under flat rocks or she will dig in soft soil, rotting vegetation or even under a termite mound to form an entirely new burrow. We have even seen females moving young from one burrow to another. Perhaps the first burrow that she dug was not suitable or the puggle was simply too large for the female to dig properly. Whatever the reason, the unwieldy move is achieved by literally dragging the young on its back as it holds to the hairs on the mother's belly. Unlike other young mammals that are dependent on warmth to thrive and grow, the nursery burrow of the echidna is cool, about 15°C (59°F).

Nursery burrows often have long curved entrance ways. The chamber containing the young is in the rear. Once safely deposited in its new dark surroundings, the female backfills the entrance to deter predators and leaves the sightless and nearly naked puggle alone. Life for the young echidna has changed. Instead of hanging upside down against the body warmth of the mother, it is now right side up on the cool earth. It no longer has access to milk at all times, but must wait for the female to return in order to nurse.

Return she does, but for only two hours once every five to six days. Unplugging the entrance, the mother enters the nursery chamber and nuzzles the young awake. Laying on her side the young has easy access to the milk patch where it suckles hardily and ingests up to 40% of its own body mass in one feeding! Body distended and tired

The pouch young's eyes are still closed when it no longer fits entirely inside the folds of the mother's pouch. Clinging to the belly hair, it sometimes drags on the ground and is vulnerable. Harassment by predators or people can cause the young to lose its grip and become prematurely separated from the mother.

When the young is about 50 days of age and becomes too large to carry, the female gets rid of it. She finds a natural crevice, a pile of composting litter or digs a special nursery burrow for the young to live in for the next 5 months.

from suckling, the young drops off to sleep as the female backfills the nursery burrow and leaves. A lactating female does not linger around the nursery burrow. She forages up to 18 hours a day while travelling one or more kilometres and making up to 1000 digs. When her internal alarm goes off, she makes a beeline back to the nursery burrow.

Exactly what the young echidna does during the five-day intervals is conjecture. Hand-rearing young has given us some insight. Once in the burrow, spines and hair continue to develop and after several weeks in the dark nursery chamber, the eyes finally open. Burrow young echidnas sleep, burp, pee and poo in their sleep like all babies,

(Above) Once in the burrow, life for the puggle changes dramatically. It no longer hangs upside down or has a constant food supply. It sleeps in the cool nursery burrow and waits for the mother to return to suckle it every 5 days.

(Right) After the young is in the burrow, the female forages up to 18 hours a day (each arrow indicates one hour of activity) Foraging takes place away from the nursery and can include up to 1,000 digs per day. Once every 5 days (white arrow) she returns to the nursery for about 2 hours to suckle her young. (Photo courtesy of the Department of Environment, Heritage and Aboriginal Affairs)

while waiting for the next feeding. This pattern continues until the young is seven months old. By this time it is completely covered with spines and looks like a smaller version of the adult. Up to now it has been living in a dark, cool burrow, totally dependent on the mother's milk for nourishment. On the day of weaning, the female opens the nursery burrow and brings the young outside. After nursing she pushes the young back into the burrow, but does not backfill the entrance. Weaning means independence for both young and mother. There is no parental guidance. A young echidna is totally on its own and must learn where and for what to forage, how to seek shelter, avoid predators and where to establish a home range.

Not all newly weaned echidnas are the same size. Mervyn Griffiths determined that the size of the young at weaning is dependent on the size of the mother. The young of one of our 5 kg females weighed 1300 g at weaning and that of a 2.5 kg mother only 800 g. Both were seven months old.

AGE, MATURITY AND SEXING

Neither size nor body mass of an echidna is related to age, maturity or gender. As yet, no one has found a reliable way to age echidnas

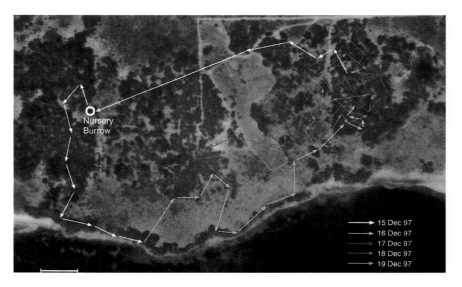

15 Dec 97
16 Dec 97
17 Dec 97
18 Dec 97
19 Dec 97

Nursery Burrow

Individuals can travel great distances at any time of year. A lactating female can be so active foraging and moving within a given area that an observer can misread the ground signs and believe there are more echidnas in an area than there actually are.

after they leave the pouch. Some researchers have used body mass as a measure of age[7,8]. Testing this method by monitoring the growth of known individuals, we find it is not accurate. There are naturally large and small individuals in the population and size is not related to age. During the first couple of years, growth can be erratic. Some 12- to 18-month old echidnas weigh less than they did at the time of weaning. Depending on the individual, there can be either large or nearly no seasonal fluctuations in body mass during the first four years. This seems to be partially dependent on how well a young has learned to forage. There are some hyperactive individuals who despite constant foraging gain little weight. These do not survive past their third year. Another influencing factor is the amount of energy spent exploring new territories as young echidnas establish a home range.

Sexually mature males show a seasonal pattern in body weight, with lowest levels reached just after the breeding period. Decline in body mass appears to be due to increased movement while males search for females, and not due to lack of foraging. One extremely active male named Casanova was found in the train of three different females over a five square kilometre area in one 14-day period. During six weeks of courtship he lost 800 grams, nearly 25% of his total body mass[9]. In any one year it is not unusual to find the body mass of an individual echidna varying 20 to 25%. Other factors influencing body mass are environmental conditions which in turn affect the volume and availability of food.

One criteria we have developed for approximating the age of unknown young echidnas is the sheath-covered spur on the hind foot. From the time a puggle is placed in the nursery burrow, this feature is prominent. All subadult echidnas, both males and females, have spurs. Spur sheaths are shed, usually individually, during an animal's first four years. The earliest shedding we've observed was in a 16-month old animal. Another echidna still had one juvenile sheath when it was four. This is very different in platypuses. The male's spur sheath breaks down and undergoes changes until the animal is two years old. A female platypus sheds her spurs 10 months after leaving the burrow. Both adult male and female echidnas can retain one or both spurs. Although we cannot use sheath-shedding to precisely determine the age of an unknown echidna, presence of spur sheaths does indicate a young, sexually immature animal that is one to four years old. In scientific jargon it would be classed as a 1[+].

Not always definable but based on objective observations, some echidnas simply look old. Features such as the thickness of the pads

We are still learning what a burrow young does during the intervals between suckling. We know that it sleeps a lot and continues to grow. Sometime after it is placed in the nursery, its eyes open.

By 90 days, the burrow young is covered with soft dark hair. The growing spines, hidden by the silky fur, feel like small sharp needles. This very round young, which can take in up to 40% of its own body mass, has just been suckled by its mother.

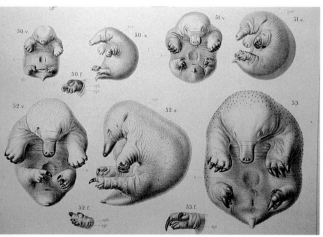

(Top) Burrow young are covered with spines but still uncoordinated and totally reliant on the mother's milk. It has still not ventured from the burrow when 150 days old.

(Above) Early researchers sacrificed hundreds of echidnas in order to produce these phenomenal works. Today, one challenge for field biologists is how to conduct their work without destroying or changing their study subjects.

and the condition of the skin on the feet, how the front claws are worn and even grey tinges in the hairs on the head indicate age, but cannot be quantified. Behaviour is another unquantifiable indicator of age. Whereas young "inexperienced" animals often show quick curiosity towards unknown objects and sounds, walking right up and poking their beak at a shoe or approaching a grazing wallaby, more worldly echidnas respond with caution and reserve.

There have been many opinions about when echidnas become sexually mature. By following individuals and establishing life records, we are accumulating facts. In January 1991 we found a subadult with one shed spur sheath. Since the young from the previous year had not yet left their nursery burrows, we knew it was a minimum of 1 1/2 years old. This animal was recaptured in 1993 but gender could still not be positively determined. In 1994 this animal was found with a train of males. A definite female, she mated and had a young. This echidna was a minimum of five years old, but possibly six or seven when she produced her first young. We still do not know if males and females become sexually mature at the same age or if the sexual bias of two males for every female in our study population is present at hatching.

I am often asked, if you can't use spurs or pouches, how do you determine the gender of an echidna outside the breeding season? Through years of field work I have perfected a method of palpating (feeling) the pelvic region of an echidna to determine its sex. Even this method is only useful for adult animals. In the wild, until a juvenile becomes sexually mature its gender remains unknown. Griffiths reported that echidnas have 31 chromosome pairs (compared to a human's 22 pairs) plus the sex chromosomes. Gender determination by chromosome analysis is still being perfected.

BREEDING INFREQUENCY

Once sexual maturity is reached, how often do females reproduce? Naturalist, George Bennett Jr. raised this question in 1881[10] when he wrote, "I am led to believe that the females [echidnas] only breed

When the mother (light-coloured) weans her young at 7 months, she simply opens the nursery burrow, brings it into the opening, suckles and leaves. There is no further parental guidance. The young must now learn to forage and seek shelter for itself.

every second year, as many of my older specimens were not impregnated nor in any way prepared to receive the semen." Bennett probably learned a lot about Australian wildlife from an Aboriginal that always accompanied him.

We have documented the breeding cycle of 25 female Kangaroo Island echidnas over seven years. How often do they breed? It is not only individualistic, but also inconsistent. Females had one, two, three or no offspring during this research period and not always with the same intervals between breeding. Only one female reproduced in three consecutive years. Her first young was killed by a cat, the sec-

All juvenile echidnas have a sheath-covered spur on the inside of the hind foot. The sheath is shed naturally when the individual is between 16 months and 4 years old. We use the presence of a sheath as an early aging technique. With time, the spur changes form or is lost entirely. In adults, the presence or absence of a spur is not gender specific.

ond by a goanna and we lost track of the third. The winter following her last young, this female died. Big Mama had a young in 1990 and another in 1993. I suspected she had a 3-year reproduction cycle and anticipated her next puggle in 1996. To my surprise, she did not lay an egg or even attract males that year. Luckily, I did not jump to the conclusion that she was too old, because in the following year she mated and had a young. This again reminded me of Saint-Hilaire's argument that scientists must remain objective, accept even anomalous facts and not be prejudiced by theory!

LONGEVITY, ZOOS AND CAPTIVE BREEDING

A local Kangaroo Island resident called one day with a report about a long-lived echidna. He said that he and his family had recorded in the farm diary seeing the same echidna since his grade school times, some 45 years ago. I was delighted to receive this information, as virtually nothing is known about longevity in the wild. I was also skeptical, as one echidna can look very much like the next. Cautiously I asked the man how this animal had been identified as the same one over all those years. "Easy," he replied, "it only has three legs." An echidna that was at the Philadelphia Zoo holds the record for the longest living captive animal. Arriving as an adult in March 1903, it resided there until its death in October 1953. This echidna was well into its 50s!

In 1997 there were 74 short-beaked echidnas in 36 zoological parks outside of Australia[11]. All but three of these were captured in the wild. Exactly how many echidnas have left Australia since the first one was exported to a zoo in 1845 is unknown, but survival of early exported animals was low.

The common misconception that echidnas are nocturnal may be partially due to the fact that many zoos keep them in the nocturnal house. This is often the only place secure enough to keep the strong-willed escape artists contained. Echidnas have been known to climb

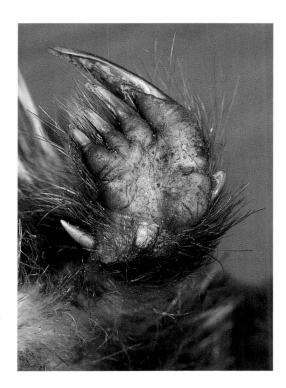

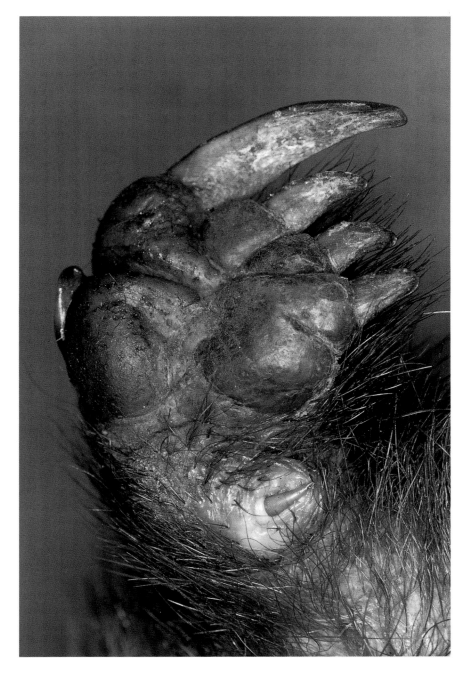

(Above) Smooth, soft skin and a sheath-covered spur that is so wide it cannot be retracted into the fleshy spur pocket indicates that this animal is a juvenile.

(Right) Some echidna feet show signs of wear and simply look old. The spur on the hind foot of this male is not normally visible but has been exposed here for measuring.

over two-metre-high wire fences, demolish soft concrete and even go down unsecured drain pipes.

What's the best time to see an echidna active at the zoo? Echidnas are shy and tend to dig in when there is a lot of movement or noise around. However, ask the zoo when feeding time is! Most exhibits can't provide enough insect mass for an animal to forage naturally, so nearly every zoo has its own special echidna diet. Echidnas learn quickly and usually become active when food is available. Food containers are sometimes placed in artificial termite mounds so visitors can observe feeding behaviour.

The Berlin Zoo was the first to report the hatching of an echidna in captivity[12]. This breeding was not planned, but simply happened. The existence of the young was discovered when it fell out of the pouch on 7 May, 1908. It died three months later. Although echidnas do not breed readily in captivity, numerous echidnas have laid an egg in captive situations. In recent years, I know of six incidences in two different breeding seasons. From these, one young is still surviving at the time of writing this book. A captive breeding program is not successful until the progeny of captive echidnas produce their own young. This has not yet happened.

There is scant information about longevity and population dynamics of echidnas in the wild. Facts suggest that some of our study animals may live to be more than 45 years old. Wildlife managers and biologists are concerned about removing individuals from the wild when a species does not breed and the progeny readily reproduce in captivity. In the case of echidnas, we have a long way to go and still a lot to learn.

ENVIRONMENT

THE LAZY GOANNAS

"At the time of the occupation of the Murrumbidgee district there lived on the north side of the goanna tribe a great hunting family known as the porcupine tribe. At the south side there lived another well-known family, emu tribe. They too were hunters, but they did not attain to the same perfection in bushcraft as the porcupines. After the arrival of these tribes from their island home in the Seas of a Thousand Isles the differences in place and climate made a change in the lives of all, and particularly of the goanna family. In their native land they were a very industrious family; they tilled the

(Opposite) Echidnas forage and travel in all kinds of habitat. Tufts of salt froth blowing off the water of the lagoon catch on the spines of a subadult as it searches among the washed up sea grasses for edible invertebrates. Fossicking near the sea is not unusual in coastal areas.

(Right) Rosenberg's goanna, a monitor lizard that grows to be over 1 meter long and weighs up to 2 kilograms, is the only natural predator of the echidna on Kangaroo Island. It is only a threat to the burrow young until they are fully spined. Goannas do not kill adult echidnas but will feed on carrion.

soil and grew vegetables and fruit. But after coming to Australia the climate caused them to dislike vegetable food, and an uncontrollable craving for flesh food took possession of them. They became flesh-eaters, and would slay and devour the smaller lizards of their own species. Sometimes it would happen that a young porcupine wandered from the cave of his parents and became lost. Like a little child, he would begin crying. Perhaps a goanna would hear the noise and would recognise it at once as a cry of distress. He would give a call, and the little porcupine would hurry toward the sound, and the goanna would pounce upon the helpless being and devour it."
—*Excerpt from a story by the Murrumbidgee Aboriginal people*[1],
New South Wales.

PREDATION

Many people believe that once spined, the echidna is impregnable. This is not true. Both burrow young and adults are vulnerable to predation. Most of my information about echidnas and predators has come from timber cutters, miners, old time fur trappers, stockmen and bush people. Their experience indicates that introduced predators, dogs, cats, foxes and feral pigs are causing more echidna deaths than native predators. In the last 50 years introduced predators are on the increase in many areas, whereas habitat change has caused

Both echidnas and island tiger snakes share ecosystems and have unexpected body temperature regulation mechanisms. We have documented that these snakes flatten their body exposing the matte black skin between the scales, tilt towards the sun and track the radiant heat to warm up.

We record presence and absence of species and sometimes even find animals by following the tracks and traces they leave behind. The rhythmic tail mark and footprints are telltale signs that a male goanna has passed this way.

Unraveling the secrets of echidna life history involves spending a lot of time in the field. I work the hours of the animals, day or night in all types of weather. Is it worth it? Reflecting on what we have discovered about this ancient survivor and what I have learned about my place in the environment, I can truthfully say, "yes."

local extinction of many native predators such as goannas, quolls (native cats), Tasmanian devils, dingoes and large snakes.

When I received my first report from the mainland about a fox "flipping" an echidna on its back, then forcing it to unroll by urinating on its face, it was hard to take seriously. However, people from a wide variety of occupations and different parts of Australia subsequently reported similar incidences, not only about foxes, but also dingoes. Once the echidna unrolls, the predator attacks the soft underbelly of the animal. Further evidence of fox, dingo and pig predation on echidnas includes reports of spines found in the predators' scats.

Feral cats present the greatest threat to echidnas on Kangaroo Island. During a decade of field work we have learned that 20% of puggles die of natural causes before they are weaned. Cats kill an additional 20% of the burrow young. Adults are not exempt from this threat and are especially vulnerable when in torpor. Besides being good hunters, cats have the ability to present their paw bottom side up with claws exposed, to the underbelly of their prey. It is not strength but timing that allows this predator to dislodge and kill an echidna. Cat kills are distinct because they leave the spiny fed-upon carcass turned inside out.

On Kangaroo Island, Rosenberg's goanna, which can grow to over one metre and weigh up to 2 kg (4.4 lbs), is the echidna's only natural predator. They feed largely on carrion, but also hunt for insects, birds and reptiles. Goannas are not a threat to adult echidnas, but may discover burrow young.

Big Mama, our largest echidna, had placed her puggle in a well-hidden nursery burrow in late October. We monitored her return every five days and I checked the burrow regularly for any signs of disturbance. In early January I saw the tracks of a goanna at the burrow entrance. Several days later my heart nearly stood still as I watched a goanna leave the opened burrow. Shining a torch down the earthen tunnel there was nothing to see; the nursery chamber was

In summer, Rosenberg's goannas lay their eggs in termite mounds where they incubate throughout the Australian winter. After hatching, the young live inside until weather conditions are favourable for them to venture out. It is ironic that echidnas may pose a mortal threat to the hatchlings when breaking into the mound to forage.

hidden behind a bend. The puggle was nearly six months old and I hoped it was too large to be harmed by a goanna. We waited for Big Mama's return.

When Big Mama arrived, she stopped dead at the gaping entrance. Beak lifted, she sniffed the air, then wandered in circles tapping the disturbed soil before disappearing down the hole. We could hear digging, and saw the earth rise as Big Mama poked her head through the ground. She was in the nursery chamber. Big Mama wandered in, out and around for several hours before settling in a nearby bush. As night fell, I crawled over and peered into the chamber. A dark spiny

Vehicles and feral predators such as cats and foxes are major threats to echidnas. Increased road traffic across Australia is having a serious impact on population numbers. In a recent nationwide survey 20% of all echidnas reported were road fatalities.

object was visible and breathing. The next morning, Big Mama was gone and the puggle was dead. The goanna had inflicted injuries to the skull and vertebra. Being too large for the goanna to eat immediately, it returned to feed when the carcass began to rot.

Tim Flannery, author of *The Future Eaters*, refers to humans as "the most sophisticated predator[2]." We do not often think of ourselves in this context, but it is relevant. We have traced deaths of echidnas to use of herbicides, pesticides and residual poisons used in vermin control. Loss of populations through alterations in habitat that affect food sources and shelter is rarely considered. Electric fences and road development are further direct causes of untold echidna fatalities. A whopping 20% of all echidna sightings from the Echidna Watch survey are road kills.

Examining road kills is not the most pleasant task, but important for learning more about physiology and life history. Living in a small community, people often bring in injured or dead animals. Many are brought in by observant children who almost always ask with anxious expectations, "Can you fix him?" "No," I mostly have to say and explain why. Then I tell them what we can learn from the carcass. This is silently accepted. "Do you cry sometimes when you cut up dead echidnas?" more than one child has asked. "Yes" I always answer truthfully. Scientists are people too.

FOSSICKING FOR FOOD

Echidnas find food using their keen senses of hearing and smell. They may also use electroreceptors located in the beak, like their cousins the platypus[3], or they may sense vibrations. We often observe echidnas walking slowly and deliberately, placing the bottom part of their beak directly on the ground. While "surface tapping" an area, they may stop abruptly, turn their head and adjust the spines around the ear opening before digging furiously and uncovering some prey.

Echidnas use both their feet and beak to reach their food. The leverage used to pry away bark or flip rocks is astonishing. The strength behind the fragile-looking beak lies in its double-wedge shape.

At the Kangaroo Island study sites echidnas feed on a wide variety of invertebrates including grubs, beetles, nematodes, invertebrate eggs, earthworms, insect larvae, ants and termites. Many of the echidna's food sources are larger than their mouth gape. We have observed echidnas placing their mouth opening around soft prey and literally sucking it in. If this fails, it uses its beak as a battering ram, ruptures the prey and skillfully licks out the nutritious semi-liquid body mass. Some volunteers equate this food source to a thick milk shake. Since many of the fat grubs and larvae are not ingested whole, no evidence of this food source remains in the scat. Presence of exoskeletons in scats does not provide a complete picture of what echidnas eat.

An echidna's agile worm-like tongue darts in and out rapidly gathering food. The powerful beak can be used to burst open morsels too large to be swallowed. Many of the food sources are soft invertebrates like earthworms, grubs and insect eggs, which leave no traces in the animal's scat.

Echidnas are cultivators. They forage in the ground, in dead wood, under loose bark, in swamps, deep litter or wherever there are dynamic ecosystems. Their activities contribute to soil aeration, spread of mycorrhiza, nutrient mixing and seed germination. Individual echidnas feed selectively, which leads to a mosaic use of habitat. Years of observations show that echidnas work an area for a preferred food and then move on to the next area before depleting the food supply. Rotating through their home range, an individual will return year after year to the same food source at the same time. Recent analysis of food value suggests that some echidnas are harvesting specific foods when they are at their highest nutritional levels and feeding on alternate species at other times of the year. We need a better understanding about the role of native harvesters and cultivators.

As the season and food sources change so do the foraging methods. Sometimes echidnas use their powerful feet and literally shred the loose bark from fallen vegetation. A by-product of this activity is more organic material added to the habitat composting cycle. We classify subsurface feeding into nose pokes, shallow digs, deep digs and bulldozing. Nose pokes are small holes poked at shallow angles into the soil's surface. This loosens the surface crust without exposing the fragile soil skin to wind erosion. A number of closely spaced nose

Although all echidnas eat a wide variety of invertebrates, individual animals may have food preferences. They selectively feed on specific foods at particular times. They seldom entirely feed out one source. Individualistic habits minimise competition between animals with overlapping ranges.

pokes result in added aeration and captures condensation within the microhabitat. Shallow digs are a combination of deep nose pokes and shallow digging action from the front feet. As the echidna moves on, spiders sometimes miraculously appear to spin webs in these digs. The moisture of the freshly turned soil attracts their prey. Depending on the character of the humus layer and the biodiversity of invertebrates living in it, shallow digs create small craters for holding surface run-off and results in a local mixing of the surface soil.

Deep digs can be major holes created down to the interface of the top soil and mineral soil layer. They often occur under or at the edge of the drip line of a plant. Generally the food source is found amongst the lower limits of the root layer. In the process of making deep digs, echidnas bring underlying soils to the surface causing them to mix with the humus layer. Some deep digs are four to six litres in capacity. Rain percolates into the humus layer but surface run-off is often caught in these mini reservoirs, providing a quick, deep watering action. Bulldozes are similar to ploughing and turning the topsoil. Depending on the abundance of a specific food source, an echidna will partially bury itself in litter and proceed to move under the surface. Sometimes they plough for a few metres then turn around and come back alongside the disturbed ground. The resulting patch can cover many square metres and look as if wild pigs had rooted there.

ECHIDNA TALK

Do echidnas vocalise? Yes, but not very often. Naturalist George Bennett wrote in 1860, "I have never heard a sound of any kind uttered by this animal." In 1865 the German animal behaviourist Alfred Brehm[4] suggested that echidnas vocalise only in very special cases, probably when feeling disturbed. He described the sound as a soft grunting. In 1970 a student from Monash University, Victoria, recorded and analysed sounds made by a male echidna[5]. He described the sound as a coo similar to that of a dove.

Echidnas show remarkable awareness of their environment. Some Kangaroo Island animals wander regularly and with ease around the base of rugged coastal cliffs. They are conscious of tidal movements and will leave the area before their departure route is cut off by rising surf.

I have heard echidnas vocalise on 12 different occasions in ten years. Though audible vocalisation in echidnas is rare, our field observations indicate there may be another form of communication. We regularly see echidnas "vibrating" and tapping objects with the underside of their beak. When a glass of water is placed near a vibrating animal, ripples form on the surface. Using specialised microphones, we are exploring the possibilities of echidnas generating frequencies outside the range of human hearing.

HOME RANGE AND SHELTERS

Echidnas have a home range, an area where they live. They are not territorialistic in the sense of "defending" this area. In fact, an echidna's home range may overlap with one or more other individuals, but there is no interaction. On Kangaroo Island, animals have home ranges of between 40 and 150 hectare (88 and 330 acres). In other parts of Australia, they range between 9 and 192 hectare (20 and 420 acres)[6]. An echidna may stay in one small area of its home range for many days or even weeks before moving on. Or it may travel the entire length of its home range and back again within a 24-hour period. It has yet to be determined if home range size correlates with food availability, shelter or population density. Once a home range is

Echidnas are good swimmers. They are seen at the beach, in fresh water dams and even large dog dishes. The beak is held above the water surface and is used like a snorkel as the animal paddles with both front and hind feet.

(Above) An echidna home range in our study site can be as large as 150 hectares (330 acres). Home ranges of several animals overlap but there is no social inter-action. (Photo courtesy of the Department of Environment, Heritage and Aboriginal Affairs)

(Right) Both echidnas and their bush cohabitants such as this Tammar Wallaby are cultivators within their ecosystems. Digging activi-ties contribute to soil aera-tion, moisture percolation, mixing humus and spread-ing of mycorrhiza.

established, echidnas demonstrate remarkable orientation and navi-gational abilities. If removed from their home range, they will simply walk back[7].

Once weaned, young echidnas must establish a home range of their own. How they know where to go or determine where other animals are is unknown. So far we have documented young echidnas using at least two types of strategies for establishing a home range. Some expand their area of exploration slowly, and others simply take off and travel a great distance in a short time. One young we radio tracked travelled 40 kilometres before settling down. It is probably important for genetic mixing of a population that the young disperse from the home range areas of the parents. On Kangaroo Island, there are areas and belts of intact ecosystems which allow echidnas to move great distances in relative safety. What is happening to young on the mainland, who must venture out from shrinking islands of native scrub and face highways, predators and vast areas of altered landscape? No one knows.

(Right) The beautifully tex-tured mallee trees provide the echidna with both food and shelter. Echidnas climb into the forks of mallees in search of insects, and some-times simply allow them-selves to tumble out into the cushion of litter below.

(Opposite) Echidnas were once widespread across Australia. Their cryptic, solitary lifestyle has made it difficult to accurately assess population numbers. Studies show that numbers have decreased since European settlement. Juveniles naturally disperse from their nursery site. Their survival is dependent on finding a healthy and ecologically dynamic living space. A face to face encounter with an echidna is a unique and unforget-table experience.

Echidnas utilise many types of habitats and shelters. An animal's home range in our study site can include woodland, open and closed shrubland, fresh water and salt water swamps, coastal beaches and dunes. We've observed foraging and shelter sites in all habitats. Animals use every available type of vegetation, natural caves or hollows as well as self-dug shelters. Favoured vegetation is dense under-storey shrubs such as *Achrotriche* and prickly acacia. This cover not only offers protection, but it is warm and dry in the winter and cool in the summer. The most unusual shelter I've seen was an 'echidna condo.' We observed three different echidnas using two different openings in a large abandoned brush turkey mound and were puzzled that these solitary animals were sharing a shelter. The mystery was solved when we excavated part of the mound in order to retrieve a shed transmitter. There were only two entrances, but inside the mound were four distinctly separate chambers! The echidnas were still living a solitary life style. At a mainland study site in central Victoria where vegetation has been impacted by rabbits, we find echidnas using rabbit warrens as shelters up to 90% of the time.

Waterways or man-made dams in an echidna's home range pose no problems. We have often radio tracked echidnas swimming across

streams. They are seen by farmers swimming across a dam instead of walking around it. Echidna Watchers frequently report coastal dwelling animals entering the sea of their own free will (not being chased by a dog or pursued in any other way) swimming out, and then returning to shore. It would appear that some echidnas simply enjoy going for a swim.

SHARED SPACE AND SUSTAINABILITY

For newcomers to the bush, living in and with nature often means an adjustment in attitude. For some, recognising that our species is just a small part of a complex system is a new mind set. "Shared space" is a concept people working at the Pelican Lagoon Research Centre quickly become acquainted with. It is not only echidnas that cohabit with bush patrons. Small migratory bats that eat insects live in the eaves of the workroom and sleeping quarters. Sleeping with a net over the bed and sweeping off the table in the morning are small concessions for having resident and ecologically sustainable "bug zappers." Besides, their close proximity allows us candid views of how bat nurseries work. Millions of tiny ants live between the walls of wooden structures. As long as their nests are healthy and active, the wood remains free of termites. This type of shared space means no poisons or insecticides are necessary. Each species usually resides happily within its realm. However, if we become lax about caring for the space we use, like leaving honey on the counter, it is an invitation for invasion. Living sustainably means taking responsibility for every action.

Echidnas are excellent models of survivors living sustainably and sharing space. They are not offensive and pose no threat to other animals. Wallabies simply look up disinterested if an echidna ventures through its grazing grounds. Curious kangaroos may risk a sniff at a foraging echidna and bound away when spines bristle upward, but they return for further examination. I've observed an echidna walking along or over a basking snake and neither animal seemed disturbed. Occasionally we find a brush tail possum sharing a sleeping

(Above) When an echidna forages at a termite mound, it usually digs around the base. In spring, we find some termite mounds with gaping holes. This indicates that an echidna has broken into the weakened part of the mound where a goanna has laid its eggs.

(Opposite) The world of the echidna is full of dynamic and unexpected interactions. An intact ecosystem has high biodiversity and is often more productive than adjacent cultivated land.

site with an echidna, or vice versa. Even though echidnas seem detached from surrounding fauna, their subtle interactions become apparent the longer we share space with them.

ECHIDNA THE SURVIVOR

The short-beaked echidna is one of only three living monotremes. Monotremes have been on the planet longer than any other mammals, over 120 million years. Monotremes and hence echidnas are survivors. As new fossil evidence comes forward we will better understand the relationship of these monotremes to each other and their ancestors.

The use of radio telemetry has allowed us to make significant steps toward learning about the echidna's biology and ecology in the wild. It is, however, the human element, the tens of thousands of volunteer hours using technology, that has brought us to the point we are at today.

Native ecosystems are inter-active networks. Curra-wongs are curious and alert woodland feeders. Their presence often tips us off to the whereabouts of foraging echidnas. As the echidna digs and bulldozes, it turns up food sources for the currawong.

Researching echidna life style is teaching us how they have been so successful. In the overall picture, echidnas are individualists. Individual adaptations of principal characteristics benefit the entire species. Echidna reproduction rate is low, they don't overpopulate and they do not compete with themselves. Echidnas feed on invertebrates, the most abundant group of animals on the earth, yet they never exhaust an entire food source at once. Echidnas help cultivate their food sources through their foraging activities. Body temperature and metabolism of echidnas has remained at a low level. This is an efficient way to save and balance energy expenditure. These are key behavioural, physiological and social traits that have helped echidnas survive 120 million years of environmental changes.

Seldom obvious within its own surroundings and practically unknown to the modern world, the echidna, a monotreme, is a living model of sustainability. These mammals have survived for thousands of millennia. Given habitat, we believe they can continue. The question remains, can we appreciate their significance in our world?

I have been collecting data now for over a decade, but echidnas can live more than 50 years. I have no illusions of being able to follow enough echidnas from egg through to adult in order to solve existing and upcoming echidna mysteries during my working lifetime. However, practising sustainable research means that studies can be continued with this population for echidna and researcher generations to come. Meanwhile, living and working in nature and with nature gives me a perspective of Echidna Time and my role in the big scheme of things. The echidna has been an active agent within the Australian ecosystems. Their continued presence may go hand in glove with the sustainability of the natural environment. I'll continue peering under bushes, sneaking around trees, sharing space and learning about the cosmos of life from the echidna, a true survivor.

ECHIDNA MYTHS AND FACTS

ANATOMY

Echidnas can bite. False. Echidnas have no teeth and their mouth opens no wider than the width of their tongue.

Echidna spurs are poisonous. False. The spurs of the male platypus are connected to a venom gland, but not the spurs of the echidna.

Echidnas have quills. False. The stiff protrusions on an echidna are modified hairs, correctly call spines.

An echidna spine can puncture a car tyre. True. If an echidna is run over by a car, the spines are strong enough to puncture a tyre, but not strong enough to protect the echidna from injury and death.

Echidna spines are barbed and poisonous. False. Echidna spines are smooth and contain no poison, but some people react to being prickled by breaking out in little red bumps.

Echidna spines can be "shot out" and inflict injury. False. As modified hairs, echidna spines have a long root and are firmly anchored in the skin.

Echidnas have three or four toes. False. Echidnas have five toes with claws on both the front and back feet.

Only male echidnas have spurs. False. All young echidnas have spurs. At sexual maturity some animals may lose one or both spurs.

Echidnas can be sexed by the presence or absence of a spur. Both males and females retain or lose spurs. In platypuses, only the adult male has a spur.

Echidnas have a tail. True. The echidna has a short nub of a tail that is covered with soft leathery skin. It is rarely seen, because the rosette of tail spines shields it completely.

Echidnas have a pouch like a kangaroo. False. The pouch of a kangaroo is permanent, forming a pocket that contains the joey. The pouch of an echidna is formed by pulling its stomach muscles together and is not always present.

Only female echidnas can form a pouch. False. Males, females and juveniles can all form what "looks like" a pouch.

Gender of echidnas can be determined by the presence or absence of a pouch. Not usually. It is only when the female is reproductively active that the mammary glands swell, forming an identifiable fleshy pouch.

Echidnas have a nose. False. No nose as we know it. The beak of the echidna is part of the skull structure, similar to that of a bird. The nostrils sit on top at the end of the beak.

Echidnas blow bubbles through their nostrils. True. The tip of the echidna beak often appears "wet" because mucus is blown out the nostrils to keep them free from dirt.

The entire length of the echidna beak opens. False, even though echidnas in cartoons are often portrayed this way! The echidna has a tiny mouth opening on the bottom side at the tip of the beak. It does not open wider than the width of the tongue.

Echidnas do not chew their food. True. Echidnas grind their food between the horny plates on the back of their tongue and the roof of their mouth.

Echidnas roll their long tongue back in the mouth. False. There are two strong muscles that extend and retract the tongue from the mouth,

The hind feet of echidnas point forward. False. The hind feet of an echidna are rotated outwards and point backwards.

BIOLOGY

Echidnas are marsupials. False. Echidnas belong to a group of mammals called Monotremes, the egg-laying mammals. Marsupials are pouched mammals.

Echidnas are related to hedgehogs and porcupines. False. The closest relative to the short-beaked echidna is the long-beaked echidna. Its only other relative is the platypus.

Echidnas are primitive mammals. True and False. Echidnas are evolutionarily old mammals, but not primitive in the sense of being basic or simple.

Echidnas are blind. False. Echidnas have small external eyes, but large eye sockets. They can discern movement, patterns and shape.

Echidnas see in colour. False. The eye is a pure rod retinal system. Both rods and cones are needed for colour vision.

Echidnas use their beak like a crowbar. True. Echidnas flip rocks, pry bark off of trees, and break open logs with their beak in search of food.

Echidna have excellent hearing. True. Echidnas have a huge ear funnel leading to the skull that gives them very sensitive hearing. Moving the spines around the ear opening helps to direct sound.

Echidnas eat only ants and termites. False. Depending on where an echidna lives, it will eat many types of available invertebrates including worms, beetles, and larvae of many insects.

Sexual maturity can be determined by body weight. False. Like humans, there are large and small individuals in the population. Weight is not a good predictor of sexual maturity.

Gender of an echidna can be determined by external features. False. All sex organs are internal and gender cannot be determined by visual inspection.

Echidnas have inferior body temperature regulation. False. Echidnas have a lower body temperature than other mammals which may also show daily fluctuations. This is a unique energy-saving adaptation that has helped them survive.

Echidnas use torpor. True, sometimes. All echidnas appear to have the ability to undergo torpidity, lower body temperature and metabolism; however, if and to what extent torpor is used depends on the individual.

Echidnas moult each year. False. Echidnas do not completely shed all their spines and hair each year. However, as in humans, individual spines, which are modified hairs are shed and replaced periodically.

Burrow young echidnas are vulnerable to predation. True. Even though the female backfills the nursery burrow, goannas, cats and dogs sometimes dig them out.

Adult echidnas have no predators. False. Adult echidnas have few natural predators; however, foxes, dogs, cats and automobiles all kill echidnas.

Echidnas can be aged by size. False. No one has found a way to age echidnas. There are both large and small individuals in a population. Even though there is seasonal varia-tion in body mass, it remains relative to size of the animal.

Echidnas have a large brain. True. Not only do echidnas have a large brain for their size, the neocortex, the part of the brain used to gauge "smartness," is about the same size, shape and texture as that of primates, animals that most people consider intelligent.

BEHAVIOUR

Echidnas are nocturnal. Sometimes. Depending on the time of year and place in Australia, echidnas may be active day or night. Echidnas do not tolerate high temperatures, so avoid the heat of the day. During the winter months they tend to be more active during the day.

Echidnas have territories. False. Having a territory implies defending an area against other animals. Echidnas have home range areas that overlap with other echidnas. There is no interaction.

Echidnas stay in small areas. False. Echidnas can have a home range of over 193 hectares (330 acres), which is fairly large for an animal with such short legs. Different parts of the home range may be used at different times of the year so an animals cannot always be found in the same area.

All echidnas act the same. False. Each echidna has a definite personality. Some always dig in or erect their spines at unfamiliar sounds, whereas others act more relaxed and are inquisitive and anxious to explore.

Echidnas are not intelligent. False. Unfortunately echidnas as often classed as primitive and therefore not highly intelligent; however, this is not the case. In conventional maze-running and tactile and visual learning, echidnas perform as well as cats and rats.

Echidnas have home dens. False. Within an echidna's home range, it may have 30 or more burrows or shelter sites that it uses at irregular intervals. Echidnas sometimes use the same shelters, but not at the same time.

Echidnas travel and live in family groups. False. Echidnas live by themselves most of the year. The only time echidnas get together is during the breeding season— winter in Australia. Then they form what is called an "echidna train," which is one female followed by up to ten males! Sometimes a younger animal trails behind, giving the appearance of a family out for a walk.

You can use a trap to catch an echidna. None has been devised yet! Echidnas are not attracted to baits and no one has found a way to lure echidnas to a trap. They are also very strong and hard to contain!

Echidnas are solitary. True. Once an echidna is weaned, it lives by itself until it becomes sexually mature. Then the only interaction with other echidnas is during courtship and breeding.

Echidnas react defensively when approached. This depends on who is approaching the echidna! Another animal in the bush may startle an echidna, but it simply shrugs and continues its activities. When a predator or human approaches, most echidnas will dig in and erect their spines.

Echidnas actively use the spines as a defence mechanism. False. Echidnas do not "attack" other animals or people and the spines are not released from the skin.

The female teaches the young how to forage. False. When the female nurses the young for the last time, she simply leaves and never returns. The young echidna is on its own to learn about foraging.

Echidnas are escape artists. True. Confining an echidna is difficult. They have been know to dig under buried fences as well as climbing more than two metres (6 1/2 feet) over others!

Echidnas stay in a very small area. False. Echidnas are travellers. Many zoos know how difficult it is to contain an echidna. Their natural instinct is to roam.

Echidnas fight. False. Echidnas are not aggressive or aggressors. When competing to mate with a female, they simply "push" each other until only one remains.

Echidnas can swim. True. Echidnas are very good swimmers and have been seen swimming in fresh water as well as in the sea.

REPRODUCTION AND YOUNG

Echidnas are live-bearing mammals. False. The echidna is an egg-laying mammal.

Echidnas lay only one egg. True. The echidna lays a single egg directly into the pouch. Platypuses usually lay two eggs.

The egg hatches 2 days after it is laid. False. The egg is incubated in the pouch for about 10 1/2 days before it hatches.

Echidnas have no teats. True. Milk is secreted from a special area called the "milk patch."

Pouch young echidnas lick the milk from the mother's stomach. False. Echidnas suckle the milk, like other mammals.

Echidnas reproduce each year. Not usually. This is individualistic and females may breed only every 2, 3 or 4 years.

Echidnas have only one functional ovary. False. In echidnas both ovaries are capable of producing an egg, but generally only one is used at a time. In platypuses, only the left ovary is functional.

Male echidnas can breed at any time of the year. False. There is a seasonal enlarging of the testes in autumn and regression in spring and autumn. Maximum sperm production in the wild is in June and July when mating occurs.

Young are weaned at 4 months of age. False. Echidnas are weaned when they are between six and seven months old.

Young echidnas start eating insects before leaving the nursery burrow. Not that we know. From observations and collection of faecal samples, echidnas do not start eating solid food until after they are weaned.

Most young survive to adulthood. Unknown. Young echidnas in a burrow have few natural predators, such as large lizards and snakes, but cats, foxes and dogs are an increasing threat, killing as many or more echidnas than do natural predators.

Echidnas breed readily in captivity. False. A number of matings have been documented in zoos, however very few have resulted in young which have survived.

Captive echidnas in the Northern Hemisphere breed, at the same time as echidnas in Australia. True and False. Echidnas in Australia generally breed in July and August, whereas those that have bred in the Northern Hemisphere usually do so in December through February. These opposite times of year represent winter in the different hemispheres; days when daylight hours are the shortest.

Echidnas are sexually mature at 1 to 2 years of age. False. An echidna does not reach sexual maturity until at least 5 years of age. It is not known if males and females become mature at the same age.

Female echidnas go into a burrow to lay and incubate their egg. Not always. Many females will walk around and forage while carrying the egg in the pouch. Some do, however, remain in a burrow.

Young echidnas in the burrow need to be kept warm and feed frequently (like other mammal babies). False. Once in the nursery burrow, the mother comes back only once every 5 to 6 days to suckle the young. The burrow remains cool (about 15°C/59°F). If young or adult echidnas are kept too warm, they die.

GENERAL

Echidnas are native only to Australia and New Guinea. True. They do not occur naturally any place else in the world.

All echidnas look alike. False. Echidnas from different parts of Australia have different lengths and diameters of spines. Density of hair, length of the grooming claw and coloration can also vary.

There are lots of echidnas. Unknown. No one knows how many echidnas there once were or how many reside in Australia today.

Echidnas can be found everywhere in Australia. Unknown. Echidnas are adaptable and very widespread; however, they seem to be sparse or missing in some parts of Australia.

Echidnas are common. True and False. Geographically, echidnas are Australia's most widely distributed mammal. However, they are not "common" as in frequently seen or number of individuals.

Echidna populations are stable. Unknown. Since echidnas are difficult to survey, there is no baseline information to compare to the current situation. There is literature that shows that numbers of echidnas have declined in some parts of Australia.

GLOSSARY

Aboriginal—Indigenous Australian people.

Acacia—A tree or shrub native to Australia, often known as wattle.

Achrotrioche—Genus of low, bushy shrubs with pointed leaves, native to Australia.

Amino acid—Organic compounds found in proteins that are essential to metabolism (the breaking of down food and releasing of energy).

Anatomy—Science dealing with the structure of organisms.

Anthropology—Study of man, customs and characteristics.

Anterior—At or towards the front or top.

Apnea—A temporary cessation in breathing.

Areola—A small area in the echidna used to describe the area of the milk patch.

Arnhem Land—One of Australia's largest Aboriginal reserves, lying east and southeast of Darwin; named after the Dutch ship Arnhem, from which the first European sighting of this region was made in 1623.

Articulated—A movable joint.

Australasia—Australia, New Zealand and neighbouring islands of the South Pacific Ocean.

Bifid—Divided into equal lobes or parts.

Biochemistry—Chemistry that deals with the life processes of plants and animals.

Brushtail possum—(*Trichosurus vulpecula*) A wide-spread Australian marsupial with a bushy tail .

Brush Turkey—*(Alectura lathami)* A large mound-building bird native to the wooded parts of eastern Australia, introduced to Kangaroo Island.

Burrow—A natural or self-dug hole in the ground used by an animal.

Burrow Young—Term for a young echidna between the time it is placed in a nursery, at about 50 days, and when it is weaned.

Bush—(Australian colloquium) The countryside in general, as opposed to the towns.

Carnivore—Flesh-eating plant or animal.

Cartilage—A tough, elastic tissue forming parts of the skeleton.

Cell—Smallest units of plants and animals that contain protoplasm, the substance essential for life.

Chromosome—Microscopic rod shaped bodies bearing genes, the units that transmit hereditary characteristics.

Cloaca—The common opening from which faecal, urinary and reproductive products pass outside the body in birds, reptiles, amphibians, many fish and monotremes.

Copulation—The act of sexual intercourse.

Correa—Shrub with elongated bell-shaped flowers commonly known as native fuchsias. Belongs to the Family Rutaceae which includes citrus.

Courtship—Period prior to mating when males pursue females.

Cretaceous—The last geological period of the Mesozoic era 100 to 150 million years ago.

Currowong—Large Australian black bird of the Genus *Streperta* that inhabits the bush and has a large beak for stripping bark from mallee trees and probing into litter and soil.

Digger—(Australian colloquium) An Australian soldier.

Dingo—(*Canis familiaris dingo*) An Australian wild dog .

Echidna Train—Courtship behaviour during the echidna breeding period. Describes one or more males following a female.

Echidna Watch—An Australian-wide survey documenting where echidnas are being seen today.

Echinoderm—Sea-urchins, etc; usually animals without arms, but with spines that are more or less globular in shape and move by suckered tube feet.

Electroreceptor—Specialised receptors, as in the bill of the platypus, used to sense small electromagnetic fields.

Embryo—An animal in its earliest stages of development.

Embryology—Study of embryos and their development.

Environmental physiologist—Person who studies the life functions of an organism in its natural habitat.

Faecal—Excrement.

Family—Category of biological classification that is between Order and Genus; comprises one or more genetically related groups.

Femur—Thighbone.

Feral—A domestic animal that has gone wild.

Foetus—The unborn young of an animal.

Fossil—Hardened remains of a living organism preserved in the earth's crust.

Fossick—(Australian colloquium) To search or dig.

Gape—Length of the open mouth.

Gender—Sex, as in male or female.

Gene—A unit that controls transmission of hereditary characteristics.

Genetics—Biology dealing with heredity and variations in plant and animal species.

Genitals—Reproductive or sexual organs of an animal.

Genus (plural Genera)—A biological classification between Family and Species;

comprises one or more genetically related groups with morphologically similarities.

Gestation—Period from the time of fertilisation to the time of giving birth or laying an egg.

Goanna—A large monitor lizard of the Genus *Varanidae*.

Gondwana—The supercontinent formed in early Paleozoic times, some 570 million years ago, by Continental Drift and comprising the present landmasses of Australia, New Zealand, Antarctica, Greater India, Arabia, Africa, Madagascar and South America.

Habitat—Place or environment in which specific organisms lives.

Hessian—A strong cloth made from jute, also called burlap.

Histology—Microscopic study of tissue structure.

Home range—Area in which an animal conducts day to day life.

Hominids—Family of bipedal primate mammals comprising recent man, his immediate ancestors and related forms.

Incubate—To maintain conditions favourable for hatching.

Insectivore—Insect-eating placental mammals belonging to the Order Insectivora .

Intraspecific—Occurring within a species.

Instrumental learning—Learning related to using a tool or instrument for achieving a goal.

Invertebrate—Any animal that has no back bone, this includes insects, worms and jelly fish.

Joey—(Australian colloquium) The young of a marsupial.

Jurassic—Middle period of the Mesozoic era representing a time between 150 and 200 million years ago.

Lactation—Period when a female produces milk to nurse her young.

Leucopogon—Shrub belonging to the heath family which produces a tasty white fruit.

Litter—A mass of organic material that naturally accumulates on the ground. Consisting of decomposing plant and animal material, it is the natural recycling bin where materials change from one form to another to return to the cycle.

Longevity—How long an organism lives.

Macropod—Greek, meaning "big foot." Collectively, kangaroos, including wallabies, are known as macropods.

Magpie—Black and white bird of the Family Cracticidae: known for its melodious calls and gregarious behaviour.

Mallee—A multi-trunked growth form of eucalyptus tree.

Marsupialia—Order representing the pouch mammals, those who give live birth to incompletely developed young, the marsupials.

Marsupium—Pouch of many mammals and the echidna.

Maturity—State of being fully developed and able to produce young.

Metabolism—Process of breaking down food and releasing energy to the body.

Monotremata—Order representing the egg-laying mammals, also known simply as monotreme.

Morphology—Study dealing with the form and structure of plants and animals.

Mycorrhiza—Symbiotic relationship between a fungus and the roots of a seed plant.

Neocortex—Part of the brain found only in mammals, located at the back of the cerebral cortex, and thought to be the site of higher mental functions, such as reasoning.

Olfactory—Relating to or connected with sense of smell.

Oogenesis—Formation, development and maturation of the egg.

Order—Category of biological classification that is between Class and Family.

Oviparous—Producing eggs that hatch after leaving the body.

Ovoviviparous—Producing eggs that hatch in the body and giving birth to live young.

Palaeocene—An epoch or division of the Tertiary period representing geological time about 70 million years ago.

Patina—Surface appearance of something grown beautiful, usually with age or use.

Pelage—A mammal's hairy or furry coat.

Pelvis—Posterior basinlike cavity and bones in many vertebrates where the legs are attached, commonly called hip bones.

Peristaltic—Contractions and dilation of the intestines, moving the contents onwards.

Pheromone—A chemical substance produced by an animal that stimulates behavioural responses in individuals of the same species.

Phylogeny—Evolution of a genetically related group of organisms.

Phylum—(plural Phyla) One of the major groups used in classifying animals, such as Phylum Chordata to which humans and echidnas belong.

Physiology—Science dealing with the functions and processes of living organisms.

Pinna—Largely cartilaginous projecting portion of the external ear.

Placentalia—Largest order of mammals known also as placentals, the embryo develops in the maternal uterus, attached to the maternal tissues by a placenta.

Palaeontology—A branch of geology which studies prehistoric life by means of fossils.

Posterior—At or towards the rear or behind.

Pouch—Temporary or permanent fold of skin or pocket outside the mother's body used for further development of the young.

Predator—An animal who hunts and feeds on other animals.

Prey—An animal hunted for food by another animal.

Prickly acacia—One of many Australian wattles which belong to the pea family. In native shrubland this spined shrub provides habitat for many small mammals and reptiles.

Protoplasm—A semifluid substance that is the essential living matter of all plant and animal cells.

Puggle—Term for a baby echidna, used as the term 'joey' for a baby marsupial.

Puggling—Verb used during the 1800s meaning to "poke out."

Quoll—Common name for a dmall carnivorous marsupial belonging to the Family Dasyuridae.

Rabbiter—(Australian colloquium) The occupation of hunting rabbits for a living.

Recruitment—Influx of new members into a population by reproduction or migration.

Scat—An animal faecal dropping.

Shrubland—Habitat consisting of shrublike plants.

Species—Category of biological classification below Genus; the basic unit of biological classification.

Spinifex—A spiny grass occurring chiefly in Australia.

Subspecies—Category of biological classification below species with distinguishing morphological or physiological differences and/or geographically isolated groups.

Sustainability—The practice of minimising human or human-caused impacts on the natural processes of the system in which we are working.

Tammar wallaby—(*Macropus eugenii*) A type of small kangaroo once common on the mainland but now primarily restricted to Kangaroo Island.

Taxa—Name applied to a taxonomic group i.e. those that share a common relationship.

Taxonomy—Biological classification of plants and animals into groups.

Teat—The nipple on a breast.

Tiger snake—(*Notednis ater*) A widespread venomous Australian elapid snake .

Tissue—An aggregate of cells that form the structural material of plants and animals.

Torch—(Australian colloquium) A flashlight.

Torpor—A state of lowered body temperature, metabolism and other bodily functions, an energy saving physiological adaptation.

Train—see Echidna Train.

Transponder—Small electronic chip with a digital code that is placed under the skin of an animal for identification. It is read using a hand-held scanner.

Troglodyte— An unsocial, reclusive person.

Tucker—(Australian colloquium) Food.

Understorey—Vegetation layer between the overstorey or canopy and the ground storey of a woodland community.

Urogenital sinus—Common abdominal cavity in monotremes into which faecal, urinary and reproductive tracts empty before leaving the body.

Vascularised—Containing many vessels which conduct fluid, usually blood.

Vegetation—Plant life.

Venom—Poison.

Wean—To stop nursing or suckling from the mother and start taking other food.

ECHIDNAS OUTSIDE AUSTRALIA*

COUNTRY AND CITY	TOTAL	EGG-LAYINGS	BRED ECHIDNAS
BELGIUM			
Antwerp	2	1	0
Mechelen	2	0	0
CANADA			
Calgary	1	0	0
Toronto	2	0	0
CZECH REPUBLIC			
Prague	3	1	0
CHINA			
Hong Kong	1	0	0
GERMANY			
Berlin	2	1	0
Frankfurt	3	1	1 from Saarbrucken 1995
Leipzig	1	0	0
Munich	2	0	0
Saarbrucken	2	2	1 see Frankfurt
Stuttgart	2	0	0
GREAT BRITAIN			
Chester	2	0	0
London	2	0	0
Paignton	3	0	0
INDIA			
Calcutta	1	0	0
ISRAEL			
Tel Aviv	1	0	0
JAPAN			
Nagoya	2	0	0
Osaka	1	0	0
NEW GUINEA			
Bulolo	1	0	0
NETHERLANDS			
Amsterdam	2	0	0
Rotterdam	4	1	0

COUNTRY AND CITY	TOTAL	EGG-LAYINGS	BRED ECHIDNAS
UNITED STATES			
California			
Los Angeles	5	1	1 (1992)
San Diego	2	0	0
Illinois			
Brookfield	1	0	0
Lincoln Park	3	0	0
Indiana			
Fort Wayne	3	0	0
Missouri			
Saint Louis	3	2	1 (1996)
Oklahoma			
Oklahoma City	4	1	0
Ohio			
Cincinnati	1	0	0
Pennsylvania			
Philadelphia	2	5	0
South Carolina			
Columbia	1	0	0
Texas			
Fort Worth	2	0	0
Lufkin	1	0	0
Rio Grand	2	0	0
San Antonio	3	0	0
Washington DC			
National Zoo	1	0	0

*International Species Information System 1997

BIBLIOGRAPHY

Abensperg-Traun M and Deboer ES 1992. "The foraging ecology of a termite- and ant-eating specialist, the echidna Tachyglossus aculeatus (Monotremata: Tachyglossidae)." *Journal Zoology* London 226:243–257.

Archer ML 1982. *Mammals in Australia.* Australian Museum, Sydney.

Archer ML, Hand SJ, and Godthelp H 1991. *Riversleigh.* Reed Books, NSW.

Augee ML, ed 1978. "Monotreme Biology." *Australian Zoologist* 20. Royal Zoological Society of NSW: Mosmon.

Augee ML, ed. 1992. *Platypus and Echidnas.* Royal Zoological Society of NSW: Mosmon.

Augee M and Gooden B 1993. *Echidnas of Australia and New Guinea.* Aust. Natur. Hist. Series, NSW University Press.

Baille J and Groombridge, B eds 1996. IUCN red list of threathened animals. IUCN, Gland, Switzerland.

Baker L 1996. *Mingkiri.* IAD Press, Alice Springs.

Baker S 1945. *The Australian Language.* Angus and Robertson, Sydney.

Bennett G 1860. *Gatherings of a Naturalist in Australia.* John Van Voorst, London.

Bennett GJ 1881. "Observations on the Habits of the Echidna hystrix of Australia." Proc Zool Soc London 1881:737–739.

Brehm AE 1865. Tierleben. Vol 2. Verlag des Bibliographischen Instituts, Hildburghausen.

Broom R 1895. "Note on the period of gestation in Echidna." Proc Linn Soc NSW 10:576–577. Buchler IR and Maddock K (eds) 1978. *The Rainbow Serpent.* The Hague. Mouton.

Buchmann OLK and Rhodes J 1978. "Instrumental learning in echidna." *Australian Zoologist* 20: 131–145.

Burbidge AA, Johnson KA, Fuller PJ, and Southgate RI 1988. "Aboriginal knowledge of the mammals of the central deserts of Australia." *Australian Wildlife Research* 1988 (15):9–39.

Caldwell WH 1887. "The embryology of monotremata and marsupialia." Philosophical Transactions Royal Society London Ser B 178:463–485.

Carrick FN and Cox RI 1973. "Progesterone and oestrogens in peripheral plasma of the platypus, Ornithorhynchus anatinus." *Journal of Reproductive Fertility* 43:375–376.

Chapman GD 1972. *Kangaroo Island Shipwrecks.* Highland Press, Fyshwick, ACT.

Clarke P 1996. "Early European interaction with Aboriginal hunters and gatherers on Kangaroo Island, South Australia." *Aboriginal History* 20:51–81.

Coleman E 1934. "The echidna under domestication." *Victorian Naturalist* vol 51 (5):12–21.

Flannery T 1994. *The Future Eaters.* Reed Books, Chatswood, NSW.

Flannery TF, Archer M, Rich TH, and Jones R 1995. "A new family of monotremes from the Cretaceous of Australia." *Nature* 377 (5): 418–420.

Flynn TT and Hill JP 1939. "The development of the Monotremata. Part IV. Growth of the ovarian ovum, maturation, fertilization and early cleavage." Transactions Zoological Society London 24:445–622.

Flynn TT and Hill JP 1947. "The development of the Monotremata. Part VI. The later stages of cleavage and the formation of the primary germ layers." Transactions Zoological Society London 26:1–151.

Frauca H, Burton B 1974. *The Echidna.* Lansdowne Press, Melbourne.

Gates GR 1978. "Vision in the monotreme echidna (Tachyglossus aculeatus)." *Australian Zoologist* 20:147-169.

Gegenbaur C 1886. Zur Kanntniss der Mammarorganr Monotremata. Wilhelm Engelmann, Leipzig.

Gotch AF 1979. *Mammals—Their Latin Names Explained.* Blandford Press, Poole, UK.

Gould SJ 1991. "Bligh's Bounty." In: *"Bully for Brontosaurus,"* Hutchinson Radius, London. Pp 269–280.

Grant T 1995. *The Platypus.* Aust. Natur. Hist. Series, UNSW Press, Sydney.

Griffiths M 1968. *Echidnas.* Pergamon Press, London.

Griffiths M 1978. *The Biology of the Monotremes.* Academic Press, New York.

Griffiths M 1989. "Tachyglossidae." In: "Fauna of Australia." Eds. DW Walton, BJ Richardson. Canberra. Vol 1B *Mammalia.* Pp 407–435.

Griffiths M, Mcintosh DL, and Coles REA 1969. "The mammary gland of the echidna, Tachyglossus aculeatus, with observations on the incubation of the egg and on the newly-hatched young." *Journal Zoology* London 158:371–386.

Griffiths M, Elliott RM, Leckie RMC, and Schoefl GI 1972. "Observations on the compative anatomy and ultrastructure of mammary glands and on the fatty acids of the triglycerides in playpus and echidna milk fats." *Journal Zoology* London 169:255–279.

Griffiths M, Green B, Leckie RMC, Messer M, and Newgrain KW 1984. "Constituents of platypus and echidna milk, with particular reference to the fatty acid complement of the triglycerides." *Aust J Biol Sci* 37: 323–329.

Griffiths M, Kristo F, Green B, Fogerty AC, and Newgrain K 1988. "Observations on free-living, lactating echidnas, Tachyglossus aculeatus (Monotremata: Tachyglossidae) and sucklings." *Australian Mammology* 11:135–143.

Gregory JE, Iggo A, McIntyre AK, and Proske U 1989. "Responses of electroreceptors in the snout of the echidna." *J Physiol* (London) 414:521–538.

Grigg GC, Beard LA, and Augee ML 1989. "Hibernation in a monotreme, the echidna (Tachyglossus aculeatus)." *Comp Biochem Physiol* 92A:609–612.

Grigg GC and Beard LA 1996. "Heart rates and respiratory rates of free ranging echidnas. Evidence for metabolic inhibition during hibernation?" Pp 13–22 in: "Adaptations to the Cold." Eds F Geiser, AJ Hulbert, and SC Nicol. University of New England Press: Armidale.

Haacke W 1884. "Meine entdeckung des Eierlegens der Echidna hystrix." *Zoologischer Anzeiger* 7:647–653.

Heck L 1908. "Echidna-Zuchtung im Berliner Zool. Garten. Ges." *Naturforsh.* Freunde Berlin: 187–189.

Hill CJ 1933. "The development of the Monotremata. Part I. The histology of the oviduct during gestation." Transactions Zoological Society London 21:413–443.

Hill JP 1933. "The development of the Monotremata. Part II. The structure of the egg shell." Transactions Zoological Society London 21:443–476.

Home E 1802. "Description of the Anatomy of the Ornithorhynchus hystrix." Philosophical Transactions Royal Society London Ser B:348–364.

Hopper K and McKenzie HA 1974. "Comparative studies of alpha lactalbunin and lysozyme:echidna lysozyme." *Molecular Cell Biochemistry* 3:93–108.

Hughes RL, Carrick FN, and Shorey CD 1975. "Reproduction in the platypus, Ornithorhynchus anatinus, with particular reference to the evolution of viviparity." *Journal of Reproductive Fertility* 43:374–375.

International Species Information System (ISIS) 1997. *Mammal Abstract.* ISIS, Apple Valley, Minnesota.

IUCN Species Survival Commission 1994. IUCN Red List Categories. Gland, Switzerland.

Jerison SM and Morgan EH 1969. "Evolution of brain and intelligence." Academic Press, San Diego/Orlando.

Jordan SM and Morgan EH 1969. "The serum and milk whey proteins of the echidna." *Comparative Biochemistry and Physiology* 29:383–391.

Kaldor I and Ezekiel E 1962. "Iron content of mammalian breast milk: measurements in the rat and in a marsupial." *Nature* 196:175.

Kennedy M (compiled by) 1992. "Australian Marsupials and Monotremes. An action plan for their conservation." IUCN, Switzerland.

Kershaw AP, McKenzie GM, and A McMinn A 1993. "A Quaternary vegetation history of northeastern Queensland from pollen analysis of ODP Site 820." *Proceedings Ocean Drilling Program, Scientific Results* 133: 107–114.

Kunzig R 1997. "Atapuerca, The face of an ancestral child." *Discover* 12:88–101.

Lancaster M and Morris J 1986. *Echidna spiky shuffler.* Rigby Education, Melbourne.

Lee I 1920. *Captain Bligh's Second Voyage to the South Sea.* Longmans, Green, New York.

Leydig F 1859. *Arch Anat Physiologie* 1859: 677–747.

Luckett WP 1976. "Fetal membranes of the Monotremata and the origin of mammalian viviparity." Anatomical Record 184:466–467.

McOrist S and Smales L 1986. "Morbidity and mortality of free-living and captive ecidnas, Tachyglossus aculeatus (Shaw), in Australia." *Journal Wildlife Diseases* 22:375–380.

Manger PR and Hughes RL 1992. "Ultrastructure and distribution of spidermal sensory receptors in the beak of the echidna, Tachyglossus aculeatus." *Brain Behav Evol* 40:287–296.

Maurer F. 1892. *Hautsinnesorgane, Feder und Haaranlange.* Morphologische Jahrbuch 18.

Maxwell S, Burbidge AA, and Morris KD eds 1996. The 1996 action plan for Australian marsupials and monotremes. The director of national parks and wildlife, Canberra.

Medicott HB and Blandford WT 1872. *Manual of the Geology of India.*

DeMeijere JCH 1893. *Over de Haren der Zoogdieren.* EJ Brill (ed), London.

Messer M and Kerry KR 1973. "Milk carbohydrates of the echidna and the platypus." *Science* 180:201–203.

Miklouho-Maclay N 1883. "Temperature of the body of the Echidna hystrix." *Proc Linn Soc* NSW 7:425.

Montgomery S 1991. *Walking with the great*

apes. Houghton Mifflin Company, Boston.

Moss C 1988. *Elephant Memories.* Ivy Books, New York.

Nicol S, Andersen NA, and Mesch U 1992. "Metabolic rate and ventilatory pattern in the ecidna during hibernation and arousal." In: *Platypus and Echidnas,* ML Augee (ed), pp 150–159, Royal Zoological Society NSW.

Nowak RM and Paradiso JL (eds) 1983. *Walker's Mammals of the World.* The Johns Hopkins University Press, Baltimore.

Owen R 1834. "On the ova of Ornithorhynchus paradoxus." *Philosophical Transactions* 124:555–562.

Owen R 1942. "Report on British fossil reptiles. Part II." Report of the 11th meeting of the British Association for the Advancement of Science. John Murray, London.

Owen R 1865. "On the marsupial pouches, mammary glands and mammary foetus of the Echidna hystrix." Philosophical Transactions Royal Society London 155:671–686.

Oxford Unabridged Dictionary 1989. University of Oxford Press, London.

Pirlot P and Nelson J 1978. "Volumetric analysis of monotreme brains." *Australian Zoologist* 20(1): 171–179.

Pridmore P 1970. BSc Honours Thesis, Monash University, Clayton, Victoria, Australia.

Reed AW 1965. *Aboriginal Fables.* AH & AW Reed, Sydney.

Reed AW 1965. *Myths and Legends of Australia.* AH & AW Reed, Sydney.

Rismiller P 1991. "Echidna research 100 years ago and today." *Australasian Science Magazine* 4:16–22.

Rismiller, PD 1992. "Field observations on Kangaroo Island echidnas (Tachyglossus aculeatus multiaculeatus) during the breeding season," pp 101–105. In: *Platypus and Echidnas,* ML Augee (ed), Royal Zoological Society NSW.

Rismiller PD 1993. "Overcoming a prickly problem." *Australian Natural History* 4:22–29.

Rismiller PD 1997. Enigmatic Echidna, Earthwatch 11:26–30.

Rismiller PD and McKelvey MW 1994. "Orientation and relocation in shortbeaked echidnas Tachyglossus aculeatus multiaculeatus." In: *Reintroduction Biology of Australian and New Zealand Fauna,* M. Serena, ed. pp. 227–234, Surrey Beatty & Sons, Chipping Norton.

Rismiller PD and McKelvey MW 1995. "Echidna research and the greater community." In: *Protecting the Future: ESD in Action. Successful Strategies for Ecologically Sustainable Development,* M Sivakumar and J Messer, eds, pp. 243–246. University of Wollongong Press, Armidale.

Rismiller PD and McKelvey MW 1996. "Sex, torpor and activity in temperature climate echidnas." In: *Adaptations to the Cold,* F Geiser, AJ Hulbert and SC Nicol, eds. pp. 23–30, University of New England Press, Armidale.

Rismiller PD and Seymour RS 1991. "The Echidna." *Scientific American* 2:962–103.

Roemer F 1898. "Studien uber das Integument des Saugethiere". 2. "Das Integument der Monotremen." *Denkschr. Med. Naturwiss. Ges. Jena* 6: 189–241.

Saint-Hilaire EG 1803."Extrait des observa tions anatomiques de M. Home, sur l'echidne." *Bulletin des Sciences par la Societe Philomathique,* an 11 de la Republique.

Schmidt-Nielsen K, Dawson TJ, and Crawford EC 1966. "Temperature regulation in the echidna." *J Cell Physiol* 67:63–72.

Semon R 1894. "Notizen ueber die koepertemperatur der niedersten saeugethiere (Monotremen)." *Archiv Physiol* 58:229–232.

Semon R 1901. "In Australien und dem Malayischen Archipel." *Denkschriften der Medicinisch-Naturwissenschaftlichen Gesellschaft zu Jena* 3:551–562.

Shaw, G 1792. "The Naturalist's Miscellany." Vol 3, London.

Smith WR 1930. *Aborigine myths and legends.* Senate Press, Sydney.

Strahan R (ed) 1983. *Complete book of Australian mammals.* Angus & Robertson, Sydney.

Temple-Smith PD and Grant TR 1983. "Spur structure and development in the platypus." *Bulletin of the Australian Mammal Society* 7:47.

Vickers-Rich P and Hewitt Rich T 1993. *Wildlife of Gondwana.* Reed, Chatswood, NSW.

Walker EP 1975. *Mammals of the World.* 3rd edition ed JL Paradiso. Johns Hopkins University Press, Baltimore.

Webster's New Collegiate Dictionary 1979. G & C Merriam Company, Springfield, Massachusetts.

FOOTNOTES

Chapter 1

1 Haacke W 1884. "Meine entdeckung des Eierlegens der Echidna hystrix." *Zoologischer Anzeiger* 7:647–653.

2 Griffiths M 1978. *The Biology of the Monotremes*. Academic Press, New York.

3 Rismiller PD 1997. Enigmatic Echidna, Earthwatch 11:26-30.

4 Rismiller PD and McKelvey MW 1995. "Echidna research and the greater community." In: *Protecting the Future: ESD in Action. Successful Strategies for Ecologically Sustainable Development*, M Sivakumar and J Messer, eds, pp. 243–246. University of Wollongong Press, Armidale.

5 Semon R 1901. "In Australien und dem Malayischen Archipel." *Denkschriften der Medicinisch-Naturwissenschaftlichen Gesellschaft zu Jena* 3:551–562.

6 Archer ML 1982. *Mammals in Australia*. Australian Museum, Sydney.

7 Caldwell WH 1887. "The embryology of monotremata and marsupialia." Philosophical Transactions Royal Society London Ser B 178:463–485.

8 Semon R 1901.

9 Griffiths M 1978.

10 Montgomery S 1991. *Walking with the great apes*. Houghton Mifflin Company, Boston.

11 Moss C 1988. *Elephant Memories*. Ivy Books, New York.

Chapter 2

1 Medicott HB and Blandford WT 1872. *Manual of the Geology of India*.

2 Archer ML, Hand SJ, and Godthelp H 1991. *Riversleigh*. Reed Books, NSW.

3 Kunzig R 1997. "Atapuerca, The face of an ancestral child." *Discover* 12:88–101.

4 Baker L 1996. *Mingkiri*. IAD Press, Alice Springs.

5 *Buchler IR and Maddock K (eds) 1978. The Rainbow Serpent*. The Hague. Mouton.

6 Griffiths M 1968. *Echidnas*. Pergamon Press, London.

Chapter 3

1 Lee I 1920. *Captain Bligh's Second Voyage to the South Sea*. Longmans, Green, New York.

2 Griffiths M 1968. *Echidnas*. Pergamon Press, London.

3 Maurer F. 1892. *Hautsinnesorgane, Feder und Haaranlange*. Morphologische Jahrbuch 18.

4 Roemer F 1898. "Studien uber das Integument des Saugethiere". 2. "Das Integument der Monotremen." *Denkschr. Med. Naturwiss. Ges. Jena* 6: 189–241.

5 DeMeijere JCH 1893. *Over de Haren der Zoogdieren*. EJ Brill (ed), London.

6 Griffiths M 1978. *The Biology of the Monotremes*. Academic Press, New York.

7 *Webster's New Collegiate Dictionary* 1979. G & C Merriam Company, Springfield, Massachusetts.

8 Griffiths M 1978.

9 Gould SJ 1991. "Bligh's Bounty." In: *Bully for Brontosaurus*, Hutchinson Radius, London. Pp 269–280.

10 Buchmann OLK and Rhodes J 1978. "Instrumental learning in echidna." *Australian Zoologist* 20: 131–145.

11 Pirlot P and Nelson J 1978. "Volumetric analysis of monotreme brains." *Australian Zoologist* 20(1): 171–179.

12 Jerison SM and Morgan EH 1969. "Evolution of brain and intelligence." Academic Press, San Diego/Orlando.

13 Augee M and Gooden B 1993. *Echidnas of Australia and New Guinea*. Aust. Natur. Hist. Series, NSW University Press.

14 Gates GR 1978. "Vision in the monotreme echidna (Tachyglossus aculeatus)." *Australian Zoologist* 20:147–169.

15 Augee M and Gooden B 1993

16 Augee M and Gooden B 1993

17 Grant T 1995. *The Platypus*. Aust. Natur. Hist. Series, UNSW Press, Sydney.

18 Gegenbaur C 1886. *Zur Kanntniss der Mammarorganr Monotremata*. Wilhelm Engelmann, Leipzig.

19 Miklouho-Maclay N 1883. "Temperature of the body of the Echidna hystrix." Proc Linn Soc NSW 7:425.

20 Grigg GC, Beard LA, and Augee ML 1989. "Hibernation in a monotreme, the echidna (Tachyglossus aculeatus)." *Comp Biochem Physiol* 92A:609–612.

21 Nicol S, Andersen NA, and Mesch U 1992. "Metabolic rate and ventilatory pattern in the ecidna during hibernation and arousal." In: *Platypus and Echidnas*, ML Augee (ed), pp 150–159, Royal Zoological Society NSW.

22 Rismiller PD and McKelvey MW 1996. "Sex, torpor and activity in temperature climate echidnas." In: *Adaptations to the Cold*, F Geiser, AJ Hulbert and SC Nicol, eds. pp. 23–30, University of New England Press, Armidale.

Chapter 4

1 Caldwell WH 1887. "The embryology of monotremata and marsupialia." Philosophical Transactions Royal Society London Ser B 178:463–485.

2 Haacke W 1884. "Meine entdeckung des Eierlegens der Echidna hystrix." *Zoologischer Anzeiger* 7:647–653.

3 Semon R 1901. "In Australien und dem Malayischen Archipel." *Denkschriften der Medicinisch-Naturwissenschaftlichen Gesellschaft zu Jena* 3:551–562.

4 Broom R 1895. "Note on the period of gestation in Echidna." Proc Linn Soc NSW 10:576–577.

5 Chapman GD 1972. *Kangaroo Island Shipwrecks*. Highland Press, Fyshwick, ACT.

6 Rismiller, PD 1992. "Field observations on Kangaroo Island echidnas (Tachyglossus aculeatus multiaculeatus) during the breeding season," pp 101–105. In: *Platypus and Echidnas*, ML Augee (ed), Royal Zoological Society NSW.

7 Rismiller PD and Seymour RS 1991. "The Echidna." *Scientific American* 2:962–103.

8 Rismiller, PD 1992.

9 Temple-Smith PD and Grant TR 1983. "Spur structure and development in the platypus." *Bulletin of the Australian Mammal Society* 7:47.

10 Semon R 1901.

11 Flynn TT and Hill JP 1939. "The development of the Monotremata. Part IV. Growth of the ovarian ovum, maturation, fertilization and early cleavage." Transactions Zoological Society London 24:445–622.

12 Flynn TT and Hill JP 1947. "The development of the Monotremata. Part VI. The later stages of cleavage and the formation of the primary germ layers." Transactions Zoological Society London 26:1–151.

13 Hill JP 1933. "The development of the Monotremata. Part II. The structure of the egg shell."
Transactions Zoological Society London 21:443–476.

14 Hill CJ 1933. "The development of the Monotremata. Part I. The histology of the oviduct during gestation." Transactions Zoological Society London 21:413–443.

15 Luckett WP 1976. "Fetal membranes of the Monotremata and the origin of mammalian viviparity." *Anatomical Record* 184:466–467.

Chapter 5

1 *Oxford Unabridged Dictionary* 1989. University of Oxford Press, London.

2 Griffiths M 1978. *The Biology of the Monotremes*. Academic Press, New York.

3 Griffiths M, Elliott RM, Leckie RMC, and Schoefl GI 1972. "Observations on the compative anatomy and ultrastructure of mammary glands and on the fatty acids of the triglycerides in playpus and echidna milk fats." *Journal Zoology London*

4 Hopper K and McKenzie HA 1974. "Comparative studies of alpha lactalbunin and lysozyme:echidna lysozyme." *Molecular Cell Biochemistry* 3:93–108.

5 Kaldor I and Ezekiel E 1962. "Iron content of mammalian breast milk: measurements in the rat and in a marsupial." *Nature* 196:175.

6 Jordan SM and Morgan EH 1969. "The serum and milk whey proteins of the echidna." *Comparative Biochemistry and Physiology* 29:383–391.

7 McOrist S and Smales L 1986. "Morbidity and mortality of free-living and captive echidnas, Tachyglossus aculeatus (Shaw), in Australia." *Journal Wildlife Diseases* 22:375–380.

8 Abensperg-Traun M and Deboer ES 1992. "The foraging ecology of a termite- and ant-eating specialist, the echidna Tachyglossus aculeatus (Monotremata: Tachyglossidae)." *Journal Zoology London* 226:243–257.

9 Rismiller PD 1993. "Overcoming a prickly problem." *Australian Natural History* 4:22–29.

10 Bennett GJ 1881. "Observations on the Habits of the Echidna hystrix of Australia." Proc Zool Soc London 1881:737–739.

11 International Species Information System (ISIS) 1997. Mammal Abstract. ISIS, Apple Valley, Minnesota.

12 Heck L 1908. "Echidna-Zuchtung im Berliner Zool. Garten. Ges." *Naturforsh*. Freunde Berlin: 187–189.

Chapter 6

1 Smith WR 1930. *Aborigine myths and legends*. Senate Press, Sydney.

2 Flannery TF, Archer M, Rich TH, and Jones R 1995. "A new family of monotremes from the Cretaceous of Australia." *Nature* 377 (5): 418–420.

3 Manger PR and Hughes RL 1992. "Ultrastructure and distribution of spidermal sensory receptors in the beak of the echidna, Tachyglossus aculeatus." *Brain Behav Evol* 40:287–296.

4 Brehm AE 1865. Tierleben. Vol 2. Verlag des Bibliographischen Instituts, Hildburghausen.

5 Pridmore P 1970. BSc Honours Thesis, Monash University, Clayton, Victoria, Australia.

6 Abensperg-Traun M and Deboer ES 1992. "The foraging ecology of a termite- and ant-eating specialist, the echidna Tachyglossus aculeatus (Monotremata: Tachyglossidae)." *Journal Zoology London* 226:243–257.

7 Rismiller PD and McKelvey MW 1994. "Orientation and relocation in short-beaked echidnas Tachyglossus aculeatus multiaculeatus." In: *Reintroduction Biology of Australian and New Zealand Fauna*, M. Serena, ed. pp. 227–234, Surrey Beatty & Sons, Chipping Norton.

INDEX

Page numbers in italics refer to photographs and illustrations.

MELVILLE ISLAND

Darwin

ARNHEM
LAND

KIMBERLEY
PLATEAU

NORTHERN
TERRITORY

QUEENSLAND

BURNETT

ULURU

Brisbane

WESTERN
AUSTRALIA

SOUTH
AUSTRALIA

NEW SOUTH
WALES

MURRUMBIDGEE

Sydney

Perth

Adelaide

ACT

CAMBERRA

KANGAROO ISLAND

VICTORIA

Melbourne

TASMANIA

Hobart